LOST
VIRGINIA BEACH

LOST
VIRGINIA BEACH

AMY WATERS YARSINSKE

THE
History
PRESS

Published by The History Press
Charleston, SC 29403
www.historypress.net

Cover images: Charles Ebbets's July 1932 photographs included several pictures of these "Dianas of the Beach" taking archery lessons at the Cavalier Beach Club. *Courtesy of the author.* The postcard of the women (back cover), mailed on July 12, 1924, was used universally to promote beach towns; the name of the town was stamped over the flag. But these marketing postcards were intended to be a happy, colorful promotional for the beach community advertised on the front of the card. *Courtesy of the author.*

First published 2011

Manufactured in the United States

ISBN 978.1.60949.204.5

Yarsinske, Amy Waters, 1963-
Lost Virginia Beach / Amy Waters Yarsinske.
p. cm.
Includes bibliographical references and index.
ISBN 978-1-60949-204-5
1. Virginia Beach (Va.)--History. 2. Virginia Beach (Va.)--History, Local. I. Title.
F234.V8Y366 2011
975.5'51--dc22
2011006809

Notice: The information in this book is true and complete to the best of our knowledge. It is offered without guarantee on the part of the author or The History Press. The author and The History Press disclaim all liability in connection with the use of this book.

Contents

INTRODUCTION

The beginning of the end is never quite where we believe it to be. Such is the story of the city of Virginia Beach. Sentimentality aside, from the historic preservation and urban and environmental planning perspective, retaining a sense of place is an important part of establishing community identity. Thusly, Virginia's largest populated city and its largest resort destination is a shadow of its former glory. For reasons not always well known nor understood, Virginia Beach has taken inordinately bold steps to bury the character and history that drew permanent residents and visitors to it in large number from the end of World War II. *Lost Virginia Beach* is the story of what was and will never be again. The pages that follow will take you back to a time when high dunes towered over Cape Henry's beach and eclipsed Long Creek and Broad Bay as sand threatened to close navigable waterways and choke the pine forests below.

Herein you will get a look at the architecture of the Oceanfront, from graciously appointed hotels to cottages, and at the people who lived there and what their lives were like before mid-century modern architecture and dramatic social and economic change swept away a genteel way of life that would never return. You will also be shown what pastoral and beautiful Princess Anne County was like before the land was swallowed up by residential and commercial development, largely unchecked, after the county's 1963 merger with the tiny city of Virginia Beach. But as was opined in the opening line of this volume, the beginning of the end started during a period that does not readily come to mind.

Surely, by the middle of the twentieth century, it was widely acknowledged that both Princess Anne County and Virginia Beach had not done enough to maintain a connection to their respective histories, some going so far as to suggest to county and town leadership that they not be swayed so readily to change place names and that, given the pressure to develop large land tracts, they spare irreplaceable old homes and preserve the cottages and storefronts that lent so much character to the Oceanfront. But stark reality stared back at those who cried preservation; many of the county's prize estates and old places were already gone, erased from the landscape and replaced by new neighborhoods and strip malls. But at Virginia Beach, it was a different story altogether. The tide of development that swept over the beach had begun not just then but rather after the Civil War, when acres of oceanfront land could be bought for as little as twenty-five cents per acre. Development in the name of progress would soon take hold from Cape Henry to the North End.

By the end of World War II, progress had won altogether. Tens of thousands of soldiers, sailors and airmen came home to the United States from duty overseas; many of them had already become familiar with Virginia Beach as a place where they had done a tour of duty, while others recalled it as a place to go on vacation leave. Still others remembered prewar Virginia Beach. Town and county leaders, anticipating the postwar business boon, agreed to pool municipal funding. Close to $2 million was spent to improve and construct a better resort for all of those "seasonal interlopers." Mid-century modern hotels and motels were planned and built. The Oceanfront began to take on a very different appearance.

Less than a decade after war's end, in 1952, the resort town of Virginia Beach was designated a city. But Virginia Beach's small-town status would not last long. A little over a decade later, small city and big county merged, an action born largely out of self-preservation. In the years leading up to the 1963 merger, Princess Anne County had lost much of its western border to the city of Norfolk, which started an aggressive annexation campaign after it adjoined all of the northern part of Norfolk County. The merger of Virginia Beach and Princess Anne County thus prevented the city of Norfolk from annexing more of, if not all of, the county, which it expressly sought to do, almost up to the day the merger was announced.

By the end of the 1970s, Virginia Beach was adding one thousand new neighbors per month. More people came at a high price. To clear the way for neighborhood sprawl, high-rise hotels and shopping centers, the wrecking ball was hard at work. Treasured landmarks and old homesteads were razed at an alarming rate. Historic preservationists and historians alike wrote postscripts for prized plantation houses and what remained of old places like Fairfield, the Princess Anne County ancestral home of Anthony Walke, located in modern-day Kempsville.

"Look closely at the small pile of bricks," wrote Helen Crist in June 1972, as it was all that was left of the once vast Fairfield plantation. "Perhaps it will serve," she continued, "as a reminder to those interested in preserving historical homes and areas here, that action is necessary to prevent total destruction of our heritage."

Gone, too, by the end of the twentieth century were places that many of you will remember fondly: the Dome; the Peppermint Beach Club, which held the distinction of being the last shingle-style building at the beach; and the Avamere, Halifax and Sea Escape hotels. As journalist Mary Reid Barrow observed in April 1995, "Very little is left along the Oceanfront that even hints of times gone by in Virginia Beach."

AT THE TOP OF THE DUNES

Antarctic explorer and *National Geographic* editor John Oliver La Gorce called it "a war of eternity." He was correct. Observant of remarkable geologic change to the coastline of the United States from the Virginia Capes to the Rio Grande in the fall of 1915, he opined that there was perpetual warfare between the land and sea, with the wind as a shifting ally. "Here the land is taking the offensive," he wrote, "driving the sea back foot by foot, always with the aid of the wind; there the sea assumes the offensive and eats its way landward slowly and laboriously, but none the less successfully." La Gorce called Cape Henry's smiling sands one of the most interesting points along the south Atlantic coast, a place to study "the battle royal" between the sea, the wind and the sand. Cape Henry had it all, he observed, "the weird beauty of its storm-buffeted beach, extending in broken masses of sand as far as the eye can reach," picked out here and there along the land edge by gnarled and stunted trees, beach grass and hardy shrubs, all of which put up what he called a brave fight against the rhythm of the sea and sand.

The coastline from Virginia Beach to Cape Henry is geographically a continuation of the barrier reef that forms the coast of the Carolinas. Spanish explorers mapped Cape Henry's coastline in the sixteenth century, and it was these ill-fated travelers who left so many shipwrecks along the Virginia Beach coast. Cape Henry was the first land sighted by explorers arriving from the south and was thus the first strand

The great dune shown here, photographed by Harry Cowles Mann about 1910, stretched inland behind the original Cape Henry lighthouse. One observer called this mountain of sand "the savings bank of the winds for untold centuries." Rising more than one hundred feet high in many places, the great plateau of its crest traveled several miles into the country, covering many acres. The sand from this dune line was rapidly filling up the Lynnhaven River at the turn of the twentieth century. The advance of the giant sand dune resembled the creeping movement of a glacier, with the exception, noted at the time, that it engulfed the forest and the river without making a sound. Harry Mann spent weeks there photographing the terrain between 1907 and 1910, and many of his photographs, even some taken after, appeared as photogravures in the September 1915 *National Geographic. Courtesy of the author.*

approached by ships entering the "great shellfish bay" because of its proximity to the entrance of a navigable channel to the cape. This bay, of course, would later be named the Chesapeake Bay, and the best descriptions of it from Virginia Beach to Cape Henry are gleaned from early explorers and settlers, men whose observations of the land and navigable waters later played an important part in La Gorce's early twentieth-century study of the same.

Spanish expeditions entered the bay each year between 1570 and 1572, sailing past the Virginia Capes to deliver missionaries sent to convert the

The Norfolk and Western Railway ran the electric loop from Norfolk to Cape Henry to Virginia Beach and then back to Norfolk again. This photograph shows a construction car of the Norfolk, Cape Henry and Virginia Beach line, No. 4, belonging to the Norfolk and Southern in 1904, the year the new service was initiated by the railroad. *Courtesy of the author.*

Algonquin tribes of old southeast Virginia to Christianity. These tribes were then part of the Powhatan Confederacy, including the Chesapeake, Weapemiooc, Secotan and Chawanook, as well as lesser-known tribes in the confederacy. Spaniards mapped Crystal Lake, a place where they also anchored their ships. A Jesuit mission in 1570, led by Jesuit priest Juan Baptista de Segura, tried to establish a small mission among the Ajacán tribe in an area he called the Bahia de Santa Maria region, near the later site of the English settlement at Jamestown, in proximity to modern-day Newport News. The Ajacáns, in their rejection of Christian conversion, killed four priests and four novices.

The Spanish tried again to reach the Bahia de Santa Maria in 1573, this time led by Pedro Menéndez Marqués. Marqués described an entrance three leagues across, with a channel following a north-northwesterly course, and an average depth on the south side of nine

Benjamin Henry Latrobe (1764–1820), arguably the best-known architect and engineer of his day, first observed the old Cape Henry lighthouse (right) after a visit to the shore in 1798. In 1879, the United States Congress approved a contract to build a new iron lighthouse (left), completed in 1881, consisting of cast-iron plates backed by masonry walls. The houses clustered at the base of the new light belonged to the light keepers and Cape Henry Weather Station (shown far left) personnel. The three-story weather station was originally established on December 15, 1873, in a one-story building closer to the old light. Five years later, the weather station was moved to its new quarters, then just a two-story work space. By the turn of the twentieth century, a third floor had been added. Harry Mann took this picture about 1907. Within three years, a large antenna structure was erected between the lighthouses to provide telegraph service for the weather station. *Courtesy of the author.*

to thirteen fathoms and on the north side of five to seven fathoms. This is a fairly accurate description of the entrance to the Chesapeake Bay, which is about ten miles across but more northwesterly to westerly than Marqués observed. An 1841 map that predates dredging operations in the bay documented the bay's depth as nine to twelve fathoms off Cape Henry, four to six off Cape Charles and up to sixteen fathoms in the Hampton Roads Channel between Fort Wool (also called the Rip Raps) and Hampton Flats. But the Spanish did not come ashore again in 1573.

Certainly, the English were cognizant of the land and bay north of Roanoke Island and the Spanish attempt to lay claim to interior parts of it. Captain Arthur Barlowe, who served as Sir Walter Raleigh's first expedition leader to the region in 1584, was aware of what the English Crown might lose if the Spanish succeeded in the establishment of a colony inside the bay. He returned to England that September with stories of "seeing Virginia," an area on maps so large that it included parts of what is today the whole of northeastern North Carolina. Swayed by what he learned from Barlowe of the region's generally fertile land and temperate climate, Ralph Lane, deputy general of Raleigh's 1585 expedition, contemplated sending his Roanoke colony north to the land of the Chesapeakes. But early English exploration north of Roanoke had only skirted the land once populated by Chesapeake Indians. Lane called the Chesapeakes the Chesopieans, which may indicate that he reached the village of Chesepiooc near present-day London Bridge but not the south shore of the bay. Captain John Smith later confirmed Lane's confrontation with the Chesopieans in a later narrative of his Virginia exploration.

John White's 1585 map demonstrated a lack of familiarity with the Chesapeake Bay. Robert Beverley's 1705 history of Virginia observed that "they had extended their Discoveries near an Hundred Miles along the sea-coast Northward; but not reaching the Southern Cape of Chesapeake Bay [Cape Henry] in Virginia, they had as yet found no good Harbour [sic]," which meant that White's party had not found the bay at all. White was named first head of the Virginia Company when it was formed on April 26, 1587, and while he ultimately hoped to start a colony on the Chesapeake Bay, he was sent instead to Roanoke, from

Philadelphia native William John O'Keefe's Cape Henry Casino opened on July 4, 1903, but most of his patrons called it "O'Keefe's Casino." O'Keefe's was built within short walking distance of the old Cape Henry lighthouse and collocated with the rail line. Though O'Keefe's was famous for its Lynnhaven oysters, served raw, roasted or fried, the menu also included Smithfield ham and other delicacies. President William Howard Taft visited the casino in November 1909. Harry C. Mann took this photograph of the casino about 1910, and Louis Kaufmann and Sons of Baltimore, Maryland, made it into a divided-back penny postcard. *Courtesy of the author.*

which all men, women and children under his charge would eventually disappear, giving rise to the legend of the Lost Colony.

Aware of the English attempt to colonize Roanoke, the Spanish pushed forward in the Chesapeake Bay. Marqués returned to the region in 1587, just as the English at Roanoke went missing, but he got no farther than Cape Hatteras. The following year, Marqués tried again, this time with the help of Vincente González, who had piloted ships bound for the region in 1570, 1571 and 1572. When Marqués and his party reached the Chesapeake Bay in 1588, the Spanish named it Bahia de Madre de Dios del Jacán; they were at thirty-seven degrees north latitude. Thirty-seven degrees is the latitude of the Virginia Capes. Spanish, Portuguese and Dutch exploration of the bay continued in the years that followed. Evidence of their success reaching the bay is confirmed by maps and nautical charts dated 1618, 1655, 1666, 1681 and 1695.

William O'Keefe would not have had much of a business at his casino were it not for the Chesapeake Bay oyster (*Crassostrea virginica*). Tonging for oysters was a familiar sight throughout Hampton Roads and most especially the Lynnhaven River and its tributaries, where the length of an oyster could equal the size of a man's foot. This photograph was taken about 1905. *Courtesy of the author.*

Despite the loss of White's colony in 1587 and a failed attempt to colonize northern Virginia in 1602, the English dispatched three small ships to the New World with the intent to establish a permanent settlement in Virginia. The *Susan Constant*, *Godspeed* and *Discovery* set sail from Blackwall, England, on December 19, 1606, under the overall command of Captain Christopher Newport on *Susan Constant* and Captains Bartholomew Gosnold and John Ratcliff on the two smaller ships, respectively. After departing the Downs Sea, Newport and the others followed the established trade route to the Canaries and West Indies before turning north and heading up the east coast, making their approach on the bay from the south. Newport's ships made landfall at four o'clock in the morning on April 26, 1607, the third Sunday after Easter. Captain John Smith was absent for the first landing, held in the ship's brig for earlier plotting a mutiny at sea.

Now more than one hundred years old, this Harry Mann photograph shows the march of the sea, driven by wind and tidal action, that carved out this trench up to the tree line. *Courtesy of the author.*

We would know little of what Cape Henry was like more than four hundred years ago had it not been for the prolific English explorers, who made it there in the spring of 1607. Struck by the natural beauty that was splayed before them, it is not difficult to picture the gigantic tree formations that prompted Kathleen Eveleth Bruce to write on October 6, 1925, that what they had seen looked like "cathedral aisles along the shore." Captain George Percy's firsthand narrative of the Cape Henry landing informs us better. He described "flowers of divers kinds and colors and goodly trees." But Newport's party, like those before him, also encountered warriors of the Chesapeake tribe who attacked them under cover of darkness. "At night," Percy wrote, "when we were going aboard, there came the savages creeping upon all fours from the hills like bears, with their bows in their mouths, [and] charged us very desperately in the faces, [and] hurt Captain

Gabrill [*sic*] Archer in both his hands, and a sailor in two places of the body very dangerous." The wounded sailor, later learned from Captain John Smith's narrative, was Mathew Morton.

Day two at Cape Henry, even after that first attack on his crew, did not deter Newport from dispatching an expeditionary party. Percy wrote that the party moved inland about eight miles, likely east of Lynnhaven. To the west they would have come upon the Chesapeakes' village of Apasus, documented on White's 1585 map, but they missed it. They also moved in a direction that took them away from Chesepiooc, the Chesapeakes' village on the west side of the river near London Bridge. "We came to a place where they had made a great fire, and had been newly a-roasting oysters," Percy observed of the scene. "When they perceived our coming, they fled away to the

Cape Henry's giant dune had one obstacle in its path, and that was the small Lynnhaven River over a century ago, when Harry Mann took this picture. Dune sand had filled in nearly half of the riverbed and would have continued to fill it completely had man not intervened. *Courtesy of the author.*

The wind cut ripples in the sand as far as the eye can see in this century-old Harry Mann photograph, taken at Cape Henry. Wiregrass, also called pineland threeawn, bends in the wind. This grass is one of the most common grasses in the southern pine flat woods and upland sand hills. *Courtesy of the author.*

mountains [the great sand dune at Cape Henry], and left many of the oysters in the fire. We ate some of the oysters, which were very large and delicate in taste." Oysters and mussels lay on the ground "as thick as stones," he continued. "We opened some and found in many of them pearls." Farther inland, Newport's men also found "beautiful strawberries four times bigger and better than ours in England," Percy opined. "All this march we could neither see savage nor town." But they did come across something else: a canoe fashioned from a single tree about forty feet long. They had never before seen any boat like it.

Arguably, the first landing may have occurred at Lynnhaven Inlet or slightly east of it. Smith's map, based on expedition findings, shows Morton's Bay where Lynnhaven Inlet is today. Three days after landfall, on April 29, 1607, Newport and his men erected a cross at the Chesapeake Bay landing site and named it Cape Henry. This was exactly two weeks before their landing and settlement at Jamestown

A storm was forming over the tall pines populating the wooded reaches of Linkhorn Bay when Harry Mann took this picture more than a century ago. *Courtesy of the author.*

on May 13. The cross-planting event also marked the first English name formally bestowed in New Virginia.

The English did not settle at Cape Henry in 1607, despite what they had seen. Cape Henry was too close to the sea and would be difficult to defend from Spanish raiders. Newport had instructions to site the settlement in a defensible upriver location. Newport, Gosnold, Ratcliff, Smith and Percy were among the first group of 105 men to settle the Jamestown colony, located upriver on a body of water named the James for King James I. John Smith cleared his name of the mutiny charge, and the summer of 1608 found him exploring the Elizabeth River, then called the Chesapeake, where he documented tall pines and cedars on the river's banks. Surely these rich descriptions would beg others to follow. They eventually did.

Though Virginia Beach today has a continuous shoreline on the north and east with inlets at Little Creek, Lynnhaven and Rudee Inlets, this was not always the case. Virginia's golden shore has changed

Before they were outlawed, market gunners supplied wild game to Norfolk's restaurants and hotels, much of it shot in Back Bay, which today is a more than nine-thousand-acre national wildlife refuge situated on and around a thin strip of coastline typical of barrier islands located on the Atlantic and Gulf Coasts. The habitat of Back Bay is diverse, including beach, dunes, woodland, farm fields and abundant marsh, most of it contained in the waters of Back Bay. Before the refuge, there were hunting clubs dotting the Back Bay landscape, including the Princess Anne and Ragged Island Hunting Clubs, the Dudley Island Club, the False Cape Gunning Club, the Cedar Island Club and the Back Bay Gunning Club. Many of these hunting clubs were founded in the late 1800s and attracted wealthy hunting and gunning aficionados from as far away as New York and Philadelphia. The market gunners in this picture were photographed about 1900. *Courtesy of the Sargeant Memorial Room, Norfolk Public Library.*

perceptibly since Newport's men first strode there. While some of these changes have been caused by devastating storm action, others are entirely manmade. Evidence strongly suggests that Lake Bradford and Lake Joyce were once part of a continuous waterway from Little Creek to Lynnhaven. The Lynnhaven River would thus have been a landlocked, narrow estuary that ran parallel to the shore and flowed into the bay at what was then and now called Little Creek when the first settlers came to live there in the early seventeenth century.

So dependent were the Lynnhaven Parish's inhabitants, most especially its plantation owners, on water transportation to reach

The Drum Point Hunting Club was a gunning club located in Back Bay. *Virginian-Pilot* photographer Charles Simpson Borjes took this picture of Drum Point clubhouse on October 1, 1925. *Courtesy of the Sargeant Memorial Room, Norfolk Public Library.*

valuable fishing grounds and move crops to market that when the distance to and from Little Creek, five miles in either direction, proved too long and often dangerous in poor weather, they came up with a shortcut. To avoid the ten-mile round trip to Little Creek, they cut a trench across the half-mile-wide sandbar that separated the river from the bay. Tidal flow took care of the rest. We know that this trench was dug before the creation of the Augustine Herman map of 1673. We also know that the inlet quickly grew to three-eighths of a mile wide and eventually eroded the point of land on which once stood Lynnhaven Parish Church. The church survived for at least two decades after the trench was cut. A new parish church was completed in 1692, and the old structure was still there, though in decline, at that time. Much of the parish graveyard washed into the river after the trench was dug, but a few important tombstones still clung to the riverbank into the early nineteenth century. Norfolk journalist William S. Forrest wrote in 1853 that, decades earlier in 1819, the inscription on an armorial tombstone was recorded before it, too, succumbed to the river: "Here lieth ye body of Captain John Gooking & also ye body of Mrs. Sarah Yardley who was wife to Captain Adam Thorowgood first, Captain John Gooking & Collonel Francis Yardley, who deceased August 1657."

No one thought to save the tombstone. The woman buried beneath it was the often married and very wealthy Sarah Offley, wife to three of Lynnhaven Parish's and Virginia's most important early men of means and power. She shared in both.

Nearly four miles south of Cape Henry, there was further evidence of another old inlet. A 1695 map in the Library of Congress collection indicates that on the ocean side between Cape Henry and Rudee Inlet was Stratton's Creek, also called Crystal Lake. This map further shows a continuous water route from the Chesapeake Bay into the Lynnhaven River, out Long Creek into Broad Bay (labeled Battses Bay), into Linkhorn

When Harry Mann took this picture of Long Creek between 1907 and 1910, he preserved a Cape Henry landscape that is no more. *Courtesy of the author.*

The blue crab (*Callinectes sapidus*) continues to support one of the largest fisheries in the Chesapeake Bay and is plentiful, even today, in the Lynnhaven River and its tributaries, as well as in the bay and ocean abutting Virginia Beach to the north and east. This picture of Chesapeake Bay blue crabs being picked for market was taken about 1905. *Courtesy of the Library of Congress, Prints and Photographs Division.*

Bay (indicated as Lincolne Bay) to Little Neck Creek and, perhaps, as has also been speculated, Crystal Lake and finally to the ocean. The 1695 map would further suggest that the entire northeast corner of the Cape Henry Desert was cut off from the rest of the county. This area was called the "Desert," but it had nothing to do with a barren landscape. On the contrary, this incredibly beautiful landscape that extended inland toward Broad Bay to the west and south was merely uninhabited, hence the true meaning of its place name. This is also the spot where Newport and his men first landed in April 1607. Here, they located freshwater springs and observed tall pines and cedars, live oak, wax myrtle, wild blackberries, persimmons and sassafras.

Eighteenth-century sailing ships anchored off the Desert and sent landing parties ashore to fill casks with bald cypress water that pooled in lagoons a short distance from shore. While the water was coffee brown in appearance, the result of leaching tannic acid from the trees, it tasted good and stayed fresh during long trips at sea. Drinking cypress water aboard ship had been common practice since the first exploration of America's East Coast. Farther south below Stratton's Creek, at Dam Neck, was another inlet and harbor at Brinson's Pond, later called Lake Tecumseh. Still farther south is Back Bay, separated from the ocean by a narrow ribbon of sand that has been punched through many times by the ocean.

As late as the turn of the twentieth century, Virginia Beach's shoreline was largely unblemished, most especially the Cape Henry Desert. Behind the first lighthouse ordered built by the fledgling United States government in 1791 was a more pretentious structure, the 1881 Cape Henry lighthouse. But the star attraction was neither. The original lighthouse was dwarfed by a great dune, a mountain of sand that eclipsed anything man-made. La Gorce called it the "savings bank of the winds for untold centuries." The dune stood more than one hundred feet high in long sections, and the great plateau on its crest stretched back into the country for several miles. He observed that this great mass of sand had slowly crept toward the interior, pushed back inch by inch by the restless wind and engulfing a great pine forest and filling up the Lynnhaven River, a tidal estuary that now flows into the Chesapeake Bay west of Cape Henry at Lynnhaven Inlet, beyond which is Lynnhaven Roads.

La Gorce called the Lynnhaven "a small freshwater stream famous for its splendid oysters." Nearly a century later, the legendary Lynnhaven, its delectable oysters on the comeback, includes its eastern and western branches—Long Creek, Broad Bay, Crystal Lake and Linkhorn Bay—and all of the tributaries. The river's watershed is sixty-four square miles. Back in La Gorce's day, the advance of a giant sand dune on the Lynnhaven was its greatest threat. To him it looked like a glacier, except, he opined, that the sand engulfed its prey without a sound, without a groan from the victim or the conqueror. Buffeted far offshore by many sandbars and reefs, the great dune had no enemies just then, hardly touched by wave action and seemingly immune to the ravages of high wind. La Gorce observed, in fact, that a good quarter mile of beach had been added to the Cape Henry shore since the old light was built.

The effort to preserve Cape Henry's rich biodiversity, first observed and documented more than four hundred years ago, began nearly two hundred years before the establishment of the Virginia Seashore State Park Association in 1931. In truth, this early effort was intended to keep Cape Henry from being swallowed up by wealthy landowners who had applied for patents on several thousand acres of land. A 1770 petition to the British colonial administrator and council of state by Princess Anne County residents, and referenced in several historic accounts that document this action, referenced "a point of land called Cape Henry, bounded on the east by the Atlantic Ocean, on the north by the Chesapeake Bay, and on the west and south by part of Lynnhaven River and Long Creek, chiefly Desart [sic] Banks of Sand unfit for Tillage or Cultivation." This was an area that was a common fishing ground before 1770. Fishermen have been described as camping in the sand hills and cutting timber for firewood from the Desert; this was, after all, how they made a living. But they could no longer fish there if Adam Keeling—whose home, Dudlies, was located near the mouth of Long Creek—and others succeeded in securing patents in the Cape Henry Desert. This was more protest than petition. Fishermen argued that patents would hurt the fishery, and thus they requested that no patents be granted so that "the Land remain a Common for Benefit of the Inhabitants of the Colony in General for Fisheries and other public uses." But their petition went nowhere just then. The Revolutionary War intervened, and further consideration of their protest was dropped.

We are left to wonder how much the Virginia Seashore State Park Association was informed of this earlier effort to set aside thousands of acres of Cape Henry as public land when its members set out to preserve this richly historic and ecologically important transition zone as a state park more than 160 years later. Benjamin Burroughs spearheaded the association's effort to keep the land from developers and businessmen who would have surely subdivided and developed it. The Commonwealth of Virginia bought acreage for the park from the Cape Henry Syndicate in 1933 for $157,000; the rest of the land

The biodiversity of the Cape Henry that Harry Mann photographed about 1910 has been preserved in the 2,888-acre First Landing/Seashore State Park. In 1931, the Virginia Seashore State Park Association was formed to create a state park. Over the two years that followed, the Commonwealth of Virginia accumulated, bought and donated land for the preserve. The Civilian Conservation Corps began developing the first 1,060 acres of the park starting in 1933; it was opened on June 15, 1936, as Seashore State Park. In 1965, the park was included on the National Register of Natural Landmarks because of its distinction as the northernmost location on the East Coast where subtropical and temperate plants grow and thrive together. In 1997, the name was changed to First Landing State Park to acknowledge Cape Henry as the first place where members of the Virginia Company landed. *Courtesy of the author.*

was donated. Over the next three years, Civilian Conservation Corps workers, largely composed of African American men, developed the first 1,060 acres of the park, clearing trails and building visitor facilities. The park was opened on June 15, 1936, as Seashore State Park, and in 1965 it was added to the National Register of Natural Landmarks because of its distinction as the northernmost location on the East Coast where subtropical and temperate plants grow and thrive together. The preserve is also a critical stop on the Atlantic Flyway. With the addition of more land and modification of the park's border with the United States Army's Fort Story, the park expanded over time and is today a 2,888-acre preserve. The name was changed to First Landing State Park in 1997 to recognize Cape Henry as the site of the first landing of English settlers who would go on to establish the first permanent settlement at Jamestown. This remarkable act of preservation at Cape Henry conjures Norfolk historian Rogers Dey Wichard's observation of many years ago that the land to which people belong always helps to form their character and influence their history. First Landing State Park is an extraordinary gift that took eighteenth-century protest and twentieth-century determination to come to fruition.

OUT IN THE COUNTRY

Just as the influence of Captain John Smith and many of his contemporaries waned in the Virginia colony, a new group of Englishmen took their place, settling in Lower Norfolk County's Lynnhaven Parish. Still in the early seventeenth century, this new generation of power brokers included Captain Adam Thoroughgood, Colonels Francis Mason and Anthony Lawson, Lieutenant Thomas Willoughby, Henry Seawell, George Yeardley, Daniel Gookin and George Ludlow. These men and many more forged a society around Lynnhaven Bay that was modeled on the one they had left behind in England. Class distinction mattered.

"It is easy enough," wrote Kathleen Eveleth Bruce on April 14, 1924, "to anglicize a country, if one [the Englishman] first exterminates all the original inhabitants, and this he proceeded to do, filling plantation after plantation with his descendants and spreading his moral standards, intent upon establishing another England in this new land far away." And thus it started. They built homes here and laid the foundation of the county's agrarian-driven economy that would prevail for centuries.

Early settlers here made their homes on exceptionally fertile farmland, all of it traveling on ridges, with creeks and swamps in between. These ridges run north to south, the best known of these being Pungo Ridge, which starts at the northernmost part of the county at the mouth of the Lynnhaven River and runs high and wide and fertile the length of the county in the Pungo section. Though Pungo Ridge is the most

All that remained of Old Donation Episcopal Church were the crumbling walls of this third Lynnhaven Parish when Harry Mann took this photograph in 1910. Located on North Witchduck Road, Old Donation was accepted into the vestry on June 25, 1736. After it was abandoned as a house of worship, the church building fell into disrepair; it was then the mid-nineteenth century. Another forty years went by until, in 1882, what remained of it was gutted by a forest fire. To preclude the church's land from becoming state property, Thurmer Hoggard IV organized and led faithful parishioners to annual pilgrimages held in the church ruins, one of which is shown here. *Courtesy of the author.*

readily recognizable, there are other ridges that played an important role in early county history, including Poplar, Black Walnut, Chincapin, Brushby, Bullock's, Eastern, Cow Quarter, Porter's and Rattlesnake. All were excellent for farming. The subsoil was clay, suitable for brick making, and nearby the forests were full of trees, good for lumber to build homes and other buildings on their land. Tobacco was the primary crop, but before the Civil War the crop selection was diversified to include hay—of which the county was once the number one producer in the commonwealth—as well as wheat and oats, among other particularly lucrative cash crops. The lion's share of work performed on all plantations and farms in the county throughout the Civil War

Richard Murray built this house in 1786 in the Indian River section on King's or Murray's Creek; the setting was very beautiful. Back in the 1930s, this manor house and all of its outbuildings, including the quarter kitchen in the foreground of the picture shown here, taken about 1930 by Frances Johnston, was the most complete colonial establishment anywhere in old Princess Anne County. In addition to the main house, there was a roothouse, smokehouse, the quarter kitchen and a large flax drying house constructed of brick. A cove of the creek came up behind the quarter kitchen, and it was there that the Murrays soaked their flax to separate the fiber from it. Other members of the Murray family had homes across the creek and also south of the manor house, closer to the main road. *Courtesy of the Library of Congress, Prints and Photographs Division.*

was done by slaves, who at one point made up at least 40 percent of the population. But not all of the county's families farmed. Some fished and crabbed, while others, especially those living farther south, produced pitch, tar and turpentine for the Norfolk and Portsmouth shipyard industry that lined both sides of the Elizabeth River and even some of its smaller tributaries. The most unique enterprise, by far, was started by the Richard Murray family: they were commercial flax growers.

Swamps and creeks separated fertile ridges, but a complex system of tidal rivers and tributaries, many of them flowing into small bays

In 1916, the third Old Donation Episcopal Church was rebuilt from partially standing walls left from the 1882 fire; a narthex (an entrance vestibule) and sacristy (side entrance for service preparation) were added at that time. The church was photographed in 1929 by Frances Benjamin Johnston. The only case of witch ducking recorded in Virginia occurred at Ducking Point in this parish in 1698 and involved the now legendary Grace Sherwood. The site of the first Lynnhaven Parish church is not known; the second church fell into the river after a canal was cut, and it washed away. *Courtesy of the Library of Congress, Prints and Photographs Division.*

and inlets, folded into more creeks and marshes. The county's natural waterways often cut so deeply into the land that the only way to move people and crops was by skiff. The first land grant on a waterway was ceded to Adam Thoroughgood, a member of the Virginia House of Burgesses. Nearly all landowners—from those like Thoroughgood with a large plantation down to the man who worked the smallest farm in the county—owned a skiff or shallop to navigate the shallows. Property owners also used sailboats and larger rowboats to conduct their daily business, from attending church or court to going to market or visiting a friend. Moving by water also helped the English avoid contact with the Native American population, which in those salad days of settlement still raided their plantations and farms. Not until these attacks stopped did the settlers start using interior roads, bridge streams and small tributaries. Conversely, they did give birth to the ferry system that has endured into modern times.

We can credit Adam Thoroughgood with the operation of the first ferry. He initiated ferry service in 1636 in what was still Lower Norfolk County at the convergence of the eastern and southern branches of the Elizabeth River between Norfolk and Portsmouth. This ferry was nothing fancy; it was a small skiff handled by his slaves. But the service was so popular that within a few months the county took over his enterprise. As it grew, more rowboats were added. This ferry service advanced through the centuries and remained in constant operation until 1952, when the automobile made it an outdated mode of transportation between the two cities. The birth of the bridge-tunnel put the last nail in the coffin of local ferry service just then.

While Thoroughgood had the first ferry, he did not have the only ferry service in operation in the county. The Lynnhaven River ferry at Ferry Farm—also called The Ferry, Church Quarter and, later, Ferry Plantation House—made an equally important contribution to water transportation on the western branch of that river, in a spot formerly called Bennett's Creek. The farm was situated close to where the first Princess Anne Courthouse would eventually be built, and adjoining on the south was the later site of the second Lynnhaven Parish Church.

After several years of operation, the court made the ferries a public responsibility. This support was made official in January 1642/3

Salisbury Plains, photographed between 1930 and 1939 by Frances Benjamin Johnston, was believed to have been built by the elder Joel Cornick in 1727, also the year of his death. Joel was gifted the land on which the house was built by his father, William Cornick, in 1692 from a part of the Salisbury Plains patent dated 1657 and from which the plantation derived its name. Joel later deeded the Salisbury Plains plantation to his son, Joel, and in drafting his will in the months before he died instructed his son to finish the house "I am now building." Salisbury Plains once stood near the Eastern Shore Chapel; the chapel was built on Cornick land. The Cornick family owned Salisbury Plains until the death of Captain John Cornick in 1859. Captain Cornick's will left instruction that the home be sold. *Courtesy of the Library of Congress, Prints and Photographs Division.*

when the General Assembly passed a law requiring that ferries be established and supported by the local population. Savill Gaskin, a familiar figure in Lynnhaven Parish, was the first to take advantage of the new law when, on February 16, he appeared before the justices to request ferry service for his part of the river. Justices Captain John Gookin, Edward Windham and Henry Woodhouse concurred that the county should maintain this service over the Lynnhaven to its eastern shore between Robert Camm's Point and Trading Point. There was no regular schedule for the service; it ran on a notice of "a hollow or a ffeir [fire]." This can be interpreted as a yell or visual plume of

The third Eastern Shore Chapel of Lynnhaven Parish, photographed by Harry Mann in the summer of 1907, was located at the far end of Great Neck as it extended south of Oceana, on land first granted to William Cornick in 1657, who had arrived in the Virginia colony in 1650. The chapel land was acquired during the postwar expansion of Naval Air Station Oceana, and in 1952 the structure shown here was dismantled and its surrounding cemetery moved to its current location on Laskin Road. The chapel was built sometime between the late eighteenth and early nineteenth centuries. The baptismal font, pews, stained-glass windows, door frames, the stairway to the choir loft and some of the chapel's original eighteenth-century brick walks were incorporated into the Eastern Shore Chapel after its mid-twentieth-century move. *Courtesy of the author.*

smoke and flame sent up by the person or persons who wanted to cross the river.

The first roads in Lower Norfolk County, later Princess Anne County, were little more than woodland paths first carved out by the Native American population and widened by the passage of oxen and cow carts used by early planters who made regular use of these roadsteads. There were no public thoroughfares and no need for any at first, not until the General Assembly passed a law in March 1661/2 requiring that a road be built and maintained between Jamestown, then the capital, and every courthouse and parish church in the

The circa 1691 coachman's house photographed by Frances Johnston between 1930 and 1939 was the last standing structure on Fairfield Farm, Anthony Walke's plantation, a vast tract that enveloped much of the land between Kempsville and Great Bridge and sat off the road, a turnpike, named thusly the Kempsville–Great Bridge road. The mansion house burned down on a windy day in March 1865. Norfolk builder and developer Woodrow W. Reasor bought what was left of the farm, a 390-acre tract, on November 2, 1967. The "little white house" was demolished shortly thereafter. Beyond the house, on a high spot and out of view, were the disintegrating headstones of the Walke family. *Courtesy of the Library of Congress, Prints and Photographs Division.*

Virginia colony, a tall order that no one leapt to initiate. The oldest public road in the county just then would be the one built between two ferry points, starting near the town of Norfolk and winding its way near present-day East Princess Anne Road to the head of Broad Creek, where the creek splits into two branches. Broad Creek was dammed in 1872 to create Lakes Wright and Taylor. At the fork of Broad Creek, the road crossed two bridges called Moore's Bridges, named for Cason Moore, who owned a nearby plantation.

A path turned road in the vicinity of Moore's Bridges is assumed to have originated as a Native American trail that extended from Little

The Adam Thoroughgood House, photographed about 1930 by Frances Johnston, was built about 1719, most probably by Thoroughgood's grandson, Adam III. The initials "Ad. T." on the west wall of the house may have been Adam III's attempt to distinguish himself from a sibling or close family member with similar initials. The house underwent major restorations in 1923 and in the 1950s and has served as a museum since opening to the public on April 29, 1957; it sits on 4.5 acres fronting the Lynnhaven River, a far cry from the 5,350-acre headright granted to Adam Thoroughgood, Adam III's grandfather and a member of the Virginia House of Burgesses, in 1635. *Courtesy of the Library of Congress, Prints and Photographs Division.*

Creek and the Lynnhaven River. This long, winding route was eventually enlarged by planters to accommodate larger carts and wagons. This area was later incorporated into the newly created Princess Anne County in 1691. The Lower Norfolk County Courthouse was also located somewhere along Broad Creek. That road from the head of Broad Creek wound its way back to the Lynnhaven ferry and parish church. Modern development has obliterated any sign of this route, but it also fanned out to the south toward William Moseley's plantation house, called Rolleston, Simon Hancock's New Town and James Kempe's and Thomas Walke's sprawling plantations at the head of the Elizabeth River's eastern

Thomas Keeling acquired a land grant in 1635 in the Back River area, now known as Great Neck Point, and it was there that this house, still standing, was eventually built. The Keeling family, beginning with Thomas, would become one of the leading families in Princess Anne County in what is now Virginia Beach, and this home would remain in that family until well into the nineteenth century. But over the years, the wrong Adam Keeling was credited with construction of the house. In 1683—the time frame during which for many years it was believed this house was built—there was no house on the Keelings' Dudlies plantation. Tree ring dating of trees felled to build the house now places construction between 1734 and 1735, a fact that does not diminish the importance of it nor of the Thoroughgood, Lynnhaven and Weblin houses, all of which have had various construction dates ascribed to them over the years. The house was photographed by Frances Benjamin Johnston between 1930 and 1939. *Courtesy of the Library of Congress, Prints and Photographs Division.*

branch. This route is traceable today despite intense development and crisscrossed roadways. There was another road, too, that branched off to Lynnhaven and traveled in a northerly direction toward Fox Hall, thus bypassing branches of Tanner's and Mason's Creeks and moving in circuitous fashion toward Seawell's Point. This is known today as Sewell's Point Road, but the northern end of it is long gone, and much of the east–west part has been renamed Little Creek Road.

Adam Keeling I left the Keelings' Dudlies plantation to his son, Thomas II. Thomas II had married Mary Lovett, daughter of Lancaster and Mary Lovett, and together they had Adam II, John and William. In Thomas II's will, dated 1714, he bequeaths "all the land I now live on which my father Adam left to me" to Adam II. The 1771 will of Adam Keeling II, builder of the house shown here, left to his grandson Adam "the plantation whereon I now live, together with the land whereon my son Thomas' [Thomas III] widow lives, together with the marsh adjoining the plantation." He also included Hog Pen Neck in his bequeathal to grandson, Adam III. The lintel of the home's fireplace, shown here, is eleven feet by eleven and a half feet of heart pine. Frances Benjamin Johnston took the photograph between 1930 and 1939. *Courtesy of the Library of Congress, Prints and Photographs Division.*

Lower Norfolk County was split into two counties with the Dividing Act of 1691, from which emerged Norfolk County and Princess Anne County that April. This was not a clean split. Lynnhaven Parish, shaped like a slice of pie, was initially left in Norfolk County. The Act of 1695 corrected the oversight and joined Lynnhaven Parish to Princess Anne County. New Town, an early business and social center of the county, was established on fifty-one acres of land in 1697.

New Town remained an important center of trade during the colonial era, but as it declined as a community, including the relocation of a 1751 courthouse, the county's trade center shifted to Kempe's Landing at the

Built about 1728, the Henley house was not as large or pretentious as Salisbury Plains. The little frame kitchen shown in this picture was a late addition to the house. Though it is called "the old Henley place" for farmer Thomas Charles Henley, who bought it in 1859 at age thirty and continued to live on the property and farm it into the twentieth century, it was originally built by Robert Mason, who willed the Pungo home to his son, James, in 1753. The property passed ownership several times, but mention is made of this house in every deed on the property. Henley had a deeper connection to the house and land than lengthy ownership: his father, the first Thomas Charles Henley, married Francis "Franky" James, on May 23, 1823. She was the daughter of William James, who lived there from 1795 to 1815, at which time the property passed to his son, Emperor James, Franky's brother. Frances Johnston took this photograph about 1930. *Courtesy of the Library of Congress, Prints and Photographs Division.*

end of the eastern branch of the Elizabeth River. Kempe's Landing, a port of entry, became an important seat of government in the old county and the center of its society. A drawbridge built there was quickly surrounded by tobacco warehouses, mercantile businesses and a well-documented trading post. A town followed. Kempe's Landing became the county seat in 1778 and was incorporated as Kempsville in 1783.

One of the finest plantations in this area was Fairfield, and while it is no longer standing, it is believed that its driveway started on Kempsville

John Pallet acquired six hundred acres of land on Wolf's Snare Creek, first called Oliver Van Hick's Creek, from Adam Keeling II in 1714, and from here he established a trading post from Pallet's Landing. At that time, Wolf's Snare Creek was navigable water that extended past the Eastern Shore Chapel and onto part of what is today Oceana Naval Air Station. The elder John Pallet left the plantation to his son, John, in 1719; he called it Wolfsnare Plantation. The second John, in 1777, divided the six hundred acres between his two sons, Matthew and John III; John III got the western side and Matthew the part with the house on it. John II's will indicated that his widow, their mother, would have use of the house for the rest of her life. Like the Keeling house, Wolfsnare Plantation was built later than the 1714–19 period initially believed. John II built the house about 1750. Frances Benjamin Johnston photographed it between 1930 and 1939. The home, located on Plantation Road near London Bridge, still stands and has been restored; it is privately owned. *Courtesy of the Library of Congress, Prints and Photographs Division.*

Road just south of Princess Anne Road. This manor house was the centerpiece of a very large plantation that extended on either side of Princess Anne Road south and west. This was the home of Anthony Walke, a man of distinction and character, whose parents were Thomas Walke, appointed a colonel by the governor and also a member of the Virginia House of Burgesses, and Mary Lawson, daughter of Colonel Anthony Lawson of Lawson Hall. When Thomas Walke died in 1692, he left Anthony I the plantation near Kempsville that we know as Fairfield. Walke's will indicated that the Georgian brick house was built between 1750 and 1770. Anthony Walke's descendants owned the home until it was destroyed by fire in 1865.

Most of the county's late eighteenth-century homes, including Anthony Walke's, reflected the growth of the planter class since the period of first settlement. A strong, diversified agricultural base made them wealthy and thus able to build larger, more stylized houses than their predecessors. Many of these early plantation manors follow the square, symmetrical and more formal Georgian plan, with a gracious center hall. On the exterior, these homes have distinctive medium-pitched roofs and minimal roof overhang. But perhaps the most distinctive Georgian feature is the use of large, dual exterior brick chimneys.

The Georgian style was wildly popular among well-heeled Southern planters, including men of means in Princess Anne County. Over a period of time, there have been a number of homes in the county attributed to the wrong style, most especially in the determination of Georgian versus Federal. Both Georgian and Federal homes can be two-story with a large center hall. Depending on the house, and personal modifications made by the builder, the confusion is understandable. But the devil is in the details. While Georgian homes are square and angular, a Federal-style structure is more likely to exhibit curved lines and decorative flourishes. The roof on a Federal home can be identified by its low-pitched or flat roof, with a balustrade. Federalist architecture was popular in the United States from roughly 1780 to 1830. Georgian colonial architecture enjoyed longer popularity; buildings from this period are found from the 1690s to 1830. Some of the most important of these antebellum homes built in Princess Anne County were both Georgian and Federal, but some of the most significant of them are long gone. One of these is Fairfield.

The story of Fairfield is a textbook case of what happens when community stewardship of a historic resource fails in the face of aggressive development. Nineteenth-century writer William Forrest described the best homes in southeastern Virginia as those "old ante-revolutionary residences in the counties of Norfolk and Princess Anne." But as he moved forward in his narrative, he really only wanted to speak

Built about 1725, Lynnhaven House is an example of eighteenth-century Lower Tidewater Virginia vernacular architecture. Constructed of brick in English-bond pattern, the house sits on a finger of land near the Lynnhaven River. For many years it was referred to as the Wishart house or Boush house. The house came into the Boush family in 1795 when William Boush, son of Frederick Boush, bought the property from Thomas Wishart and Porcia, his wife, at Little Creek off what is today Independence Boulevard on Wishart Road in Virginia Beach. Frances Johnston photographed the house between 1930 and 1939, after the roof changed. *Courtesy of the Library of Congress, Prints and Photographs Division.*

of one in the vicinity of Kempsville, about ten miles from Norfolk, that belonged to the descendants of Anthony Walke, one of the county's early settlers. The land on which this house was built was purchased in 1697. The entrance to the property was described as half a mile from Kempsville, with the old mansion set about a quarter of a mile from the entrance to the Kempsville–Great Bridge road. "This Dutch roof relic of antiquity," he called it, had walls more than four feet thick for some distance above the ground. The interior walls and ceilings were heavily adorned with wainscoting constructed of black walnut, and its passage exceeded any description of spacious, dotted as it was with architectural

The first Thurmer Hoggard built Poplar Hall sometime between 1761 and 1767 on the first parcel of land he acquired in old Princess Anne County for his plantation; he eventually owned 1,083 acres. Poplar Hall, shown here about 1900, was built of Flemish-bond brick, still stands at the western end of Poplar Hall Drive and is now within the boundary of the city of Norfolk. The house was named for the row of Lombardy poplars brought from England and planted between the house and creek. Hoggard also had a shipbuilding business that he operated from Broad Creek in front of the house at the end of the eighteenth century, and for many years after this operation ended, remnants of it were still visible at low tide. This shipyard is believed to be the first navy yard in America. *Courtesy of the author.*

flourishes uncommon in county manor homes of the period. Walke had built the house with brick from England, and with marble mantels, a brass door knocker and doorknobs.

An old Princess Anne farmer and storekeeper, John Ivy Herrick—in fact one of the oldest residents in the county when he died in 1931 at age eighty—described the hugeness of the parlor and noted the coat of arms over a hand-carved mantelpiece in the dining room. When they spoke to Herrick for their 1931 narrative on old Princess Anne County homes, Sadie Scott and Vernon Hope Kellam observed that Herrick faltered and then said, "I've been in all the rooms. I was at the funeral of David Walke." Fairfield has been further described as an almost baronial establishment, with liveried black servants, as well as blacksmiths, wagon makers, saddlers and tradesmen brought from England to ply their trades.

Anthony Walke died on November 8, 1768, at Fairfield and was laid to rest in the family cemetery on the ridge behind the house. From Walke family historian Calvert Walke "Bill" Tazewell, we know that the burying ground at Fairfield was about two hundred yards from what we will learn in the narrative to follow was the coachman's house and perhaps other servants' quarters behind the manor house. The cemetery ran to the rear and right of it. This reverent space was at one time enclosed by a brick wall, which had long since disappeared when the property was acquired for development centuries later. Horatio Cornick Hoggard told Tazewell that the Fairfield property passed out of Walke ownership to a man named Sanderlin. Jonathan Sanderlin was a native North Carolinian who farmed the old Walke plantation until his death after the turn of the twentieth century; his family continued to farm it several years after he died. Sanderlin used the cemetery wall to enclose his hogs; Tazewell observed that this had uprooted many of the Walke tombstones. Anthony Walke's headstone was particularly elaborate for its period and had been fashioned from marble. Tazewell noted, too, that it had very heavy marble foundations, probably a single slab. On the upright side was another slab with an inscription. Perhaps the weight and ground settlement did the damage, or maybe it was the hogs, but the foundation of his tomb had sunken into the ground. If it had been one slab, it was now broken, the inscription in three parts but still legible. Tazewell recorded it thusly:

Peter Singleton I's Kempsville home, Pleasant Hall, is Georgian architecture of the second period and inscribed with the date 1779. Further research indicates, however, that British Loyalist George Logan may actually have built the house between 1769 and 1770; Logan also built a new mercantile just east of the house at that time. Frances Benjamin Johnston took this picture of Pleasant Hall before November 1929, when the Daughters of the American Revolution erected a historic marker outside the fence in front of the house to document the November 15, 1775 skirmish at Kempsville that left minuteman John Ackiss dead and the British with a victory. Logan announced his support for the Crown and promptly returned to Scotland; John Murray, Lord Dunmore, briefly used Logan's home as his headquarters. *Courtesy of the Library of Congress, Prints and Photographs Division.*

To the Memory of
Coll. A N T H O N Y   W A L K E
a sincere Friend & chearful Companion
Steady in the practice of Christianity
and a Zealous promoter of Virtue
he was for many Years a Member
of the Houfe of Burgeffes
and Judge of the Court of this County
in his public capacity he behaved himself
with an Uniform regard to Justice
tempered with Mercy and in all reffects
confulted the Interests of the County
over which he prefided

he died the 8th day of November 1768
in the 76 Year of his Age

Near a cemetery tree was a grave with brick sides and a flat slab on top, which Tazewell believed was the grave of one of Anthony Walke's wives. But the inscription was illegible, eaten away by the centuries of wind and weather. Nearby was the grave of David Walke, marked by a shaft and enclosed by an iron fence. His inscription was long and poignant, more detailed than many that Tazewell recorded on his visit:

M E M E N T O   O F
D A V I D   M.   W A L K E
WHO WAS BORN ON THE 26ᵀᴴ DAY OF JANUARY
1800 AND DEPARTED THIS LIFE ON THE 9TH
DAY OF JUNE 1854

He was a firm believer in Christianity
and in the Holy Scriptures, but
acknowledges with shame having
fallen far short of living in
strict obedience to its holy
precepts and commandments.

Built before 1800, the home of Henry Thomas Cornick Jr. was located to the rear of a home occupied by Mary Frances "Fannie" Colonna, whose mother was Cornick's daughter, Mary Olivia "Mollie" Cornick. Mollie married George Washington Fentress, son of Lancaster and Diana Munden Fentress, and Fannie was born in October 1879, named for Henry Cornick's wife and her grandmother. Henry Cornick was born in Princess Anne County in 1814 and died there in 1892. The house was photographed about 1925. *Courtesy of the Library of Congress, Prints and Photographs Division.*

The world can never give
The bliss for which we sigh,
'Tis not the whole of life to live,
Nor all of death to die.

Beyond this vale of tears
There is a life above,
Unmeasured by the flight of years,
And all that life is love.

Oh could we make our doubts remove-
Those gloomy doubts that rise,
And see the Canaan that we love,
With faith's illumined eyes-

Could we but climb where Moses stood,
And view the landscape o'er-
Not Jordan's stream, not death's cold flood
Should fright us from the shore.

These were beautifully wrought words to honor a life well lived. Tazewell recorded as many of the tombstones as he could make out; he knew that they might be gone soon. Aside from special tombstones that he observed and described behind the coachman's house, of which Anthony's and David Walke's were two, all of the rest were marble upright slabs, measuring three to four feet high. There would normally be no need to repeat a full inscription here, but time and experience learning after the fact that another historic property, including its family cemetery, has been bulldozed before anyone knew it was there is reason enough to remind us all that these were our ancestors and that without them and their forward progress at another time we would not be here. The graves at Fairfield, at least in part, were ultimately relocated to Old Donation Church.

Storekeeper John Herrick told passersby in the fall of 1914 that just before the end of the Civil War a fire started in a pine wood between Kempsville and Fairfield. The fire got quickly out of control and destroyed the mansion. Another account of the fire stated that it happened in March 1865, when a spark from the chimney set the roof on fire. But the latter account was unattributed. Herrick lived in an imposing brick house, set back in a grove of trees that county legend indicated had been the home of Kempsville Tory George Logan, who entertained John Murray, Lord Dunmore, Virginia's last royal governor. This would be the late Peter Singleton I's Pleasant Hall. As a young man, Herrick was thus living in proximity when the actual fire took place and was old enough at the time it occurred to remember the night it happened.

The Croatan Club was a private hunting and fishing lodge south of Virginia Beach's Rudee Inlet. The club derived its name from an area of present-day Virginia Beach also called Croatan, named for the word C-R-O-A-T-O-A-N carved into a fort post and the letters C-R-O into a nearby tree by a member of the Lost Colony, an English settlement established just south of this location on North Carolina's Roanoke Island in 1587. The Roanoke settlers referred to Hatteras Island as Croatoan Island, thus it was later believed that the colonists might have fled there under the protection of Manteo and carved the name in the post to ostensibly alert returning expedition leader John White to their location when he later returned to the colony, which he did not do until 1590. But as fortune would have it, a hurricane off the Outer Banks forced White's return to England; he never set foot on the island again. The colonists were thereafter considered "lost," although no one could conclusively prove their whereabouts just then. Henry William Gillen, founder of Norfolk's Acme Photo Company, took this picture in 1928. *Courtesy of the author.*

Regardless, all that was left after the smoke cleared were a few outbuildings, including what for many years had been described as the kitchen. But this was actually more likely the coachman's house. Some have speculated that it might also have been part of a complex of servants' quarters. At the beginning of the twentieth century, this was the only "house" remaining on the property, occupied just then by an African American overseer and his family. Across the Kempsville–

Frank Kellam replaced Reuben Lovett's residence with this brick home, photographed by Frances Benjamin Johnston between 1933 and 1939. *Courtesy of the Library of Congress, Prints and Photographs Division.*

Great Bridge road was a large brick home that once belonged to James Walke. The coachman's house, also referred to affectionately as "the little white house," was allowed to deteriorate over time.

"It really doesn't look like much any more," opined Helen Crist, writing about the house on February 17, 1972. She described wide holes in the steep roof and weeds growing high around the structure. The house as it was then bore no resemblance to the house that Crist and others had visited just two years before. Worse yet, she wrote, "its fate was doubtful then, as new homes sprang up like mushrooms in Kempsville. There were many then who wondered what would become of the historical house." This "little gem of a house" was a one-and-a-half-story, sharp-roof building made of hand-molded bricks laid in the Flemish bond method. In its later life, the house was whitewashed, making this feature

The fourth Princess Anne County Courthouse, authorized in 1782 and completed five years later, was located on State Route 165, Princess Anne Road, which becomes North Landing Road at the "cross roads." The building shown here served as the county court from 1787 to 1823–24, when a new court building was built at the "cross roads," the location of today's Virginia Beach Municipal Center. After its abandonment, the old brick courthouse served as the home of Kempsville Baptist Church from 1826 to 1911. The building was razed in November 1971. *Courtesy of the Library of Congress, Prints and Photographs Division.*

unnoticeable. But more importantly, it was all that was left of Fairfield, the plantation that was just as significant in those salad days of the county as those with names like Lawson Hall, Greenwich and Rolleston.

At one point, Crist and little white house supporters all believed that developer Woodrow W. Reasor—who had bought the 390-acre tract in November 1967 from the heirs of James Carey Hudgins for slightly more than $1.5 million—might renovate it; after all, he had already begun the process but had suddenly stopped. What was left, she observed, was "an embarrassment to us all, because it stands as a monument to the past about which nobody did anything. There are those who look at it, shaking their heads and feeling somehow, a sense of guilt, a guilt of omission."

Reasor's role in preservation of the little white house is spotty. "I bent over backwards," he told Crist, "on this house. I offered it a year ago [1971] to the historical society for $10,000, the price of the lot, if they would restore it." The historical society did not have the money, he said. The upshot of Reasor's story, later learned by Crist, was that he never made such an offer to the historical society and the society never contacted him to make an offer. Reasor was ultimately unsuccessful in finding a buyer for the little white house at Fairfield. He built the Fairfield neighborhood over the footprint of Anthony Walke's plantation, including the little white house. This Virginia Beach development today lies on the west side of Kempsville Road, south of Kemps Landing Elementary School and north of Kempsville Colony subdivision; it also extends west to a finger of the eastern branch of the Elizabeth River. This neighborhood, too, is the textbook example of a residential development laid out in a complex pattern of streets that defy logic. The development is filled with curved streets and cul-de-sacs that fan out at irregular intervals to cut down on traffic noise and to divert the view of passersby from looking at one house and yard after another.

The loss of the last bit of Fairfield was tragic. But sometimes saving the main structure on a historic property does not preserve the historic landscape—the property that envelops the house and on which there were additional quarters, carriage houses, barns and support structures. This was the case with the aforementioned Ferry Farm, situated on land that played an important role in Princess Anne County history from the 1600s, and which is only half to three-quarters of a mile from Old Donation Church. Thomas Martin sold the Ferry Farm to Anthony Walke II, who eventually willed a larger property to his son, William, who married Mary Calvert. From historic records, we know that the third courthouse, also the first brick courthouse in the county, was collocated here with the 1751 Walke mansion, built in the lifetime of William Walke and tragically destroyed by fire in 1828. William Walke died on January 1, 1795, and was buried a few hundred yards from this house. The current house, now called Ferry Plantation House, dates to about 1830. Today, we appreciate the remaining home as an excellent example of Federal farmhouse architecture built by slave labor and once covered in a sheath of oyster shell stucco. This home was partly rebuilt with bricks salvaged from the ruins of the Walke manor.

The State Agricultural Board chose a site off the Little Creek Reservoir and the Norfolk and Southern Railroad right of way to locate an agricultural experimentation station in August 1906. After the Civil War, Virginia fruit and vegetable growers held an advantage getting crops to market in the North, and business was booming. But with its success, the state was also experiencing an increase in crop disease and insect infestation. The Southern Produce Company, an organization of truck crop growers and market gardeners from Norfolk, took the first step to establish Virginia Truck Experiment Station, which it was called from 1907 to 1967. The station's first staff, pictured in 1909, consisted of (left to right) Joseph Milstead, United States Department of Agriculture (USDA); C.S. Heller; Monnie Leatherbury, secretary; Thomas C. Johnson, a chemist and the center's first director; and Alfred Orcutt, USDA. Today the station is known as the Hampton Roads Agricultural Research and Extension Center. *Courtesy of the Hampton Roads Agricultural Research and Extension Center.*

Fast forward more than 150 years. Situated on a thirty-three-acre peninsula at the end of Pembroke Boulevard, the farm became the target of an upscale residential development. Two developers, F. Donald Reid and Jerry Womack, planned to build thirty-nine single-family homes on the site that they had bought in late 1986 from the estate of Ethel H. Howren. Reid, who was also a member of the Virginia Beach Planning Commission, took advantage of a new open-space zoning law that made it feasible for him to retain the Ferry Plantation House and a limited amount of space around it. When the city council initially approved

Reid and Womack's subdivision plan, it required that the house not be demolished or used as a residence, that a long-term use and maintenance plan be developed and that four acres of open space around it be declared a city historical and cultural district. According to a September 10, 1987 *Ledger-Star* report, before the rest of the farm was bulldozed and built up they agreed to hosting and then financed archaeologists from Colonial Williamsburg Foundation to document the site. What they found was extraordinary. "We have rarely, if ever, come across such a well preserved volume of material," according to Dr. Marley R. Brown III, today the director of archaeological excavation and conservation in Williamsburg. "Hopefully, this site will communicate how important such findings can be." The Ferry Farm property turned out to be one of the best archaeological finds in Hampton Roads.

"I hope that the planning department and the city can work on a more comprehensive and systematic approach," Brown continued, speaking of the need to identify and save historic sites. Another state archaeologist, Dr. E. Randolph Turner III, now director of the Virginia Department of Historic Resources Tidewater Regional Office, agreed. He believed that what made Ferry Farm so unusual was not its setting but rather the fact that it was excavated at all. "What you have here is a time capsule." The archaeological dig at Ferry Farm produced more than fifty thousand artifacts, including pieces of European pottery, locks, keys, coins, bottles, animal bones and utensils. They also located the filled-in basement near the manor house that is believed to be the remains of an eighteenth-century tavern that once stood near the courthouse. Archaeologists could tell by what they unearthed that tavern owner Anthony Walke II was wealthy because of the pieces of expensive porcelain and bone-handled utensils they found. Knives and forks, they observed, were relatively rare in the colonial period, thus "a bone-handled set would have been a big deal," Brown observed. Certainly, those involved in the Ferry Farm dig hoped that their findings would encourage the City of Virginia Beach to consider a local historic preservation law. Rob Hunter, the head of the dig, agreed. "The rest of the community now sees that archaeology is not the main obstacle to development," he remarked. "It can enhance the value of a property."

After the dig was completed, the tavern basement was refilled and a road built over it. The tens of thousands of artifacts pulled from the

The Keystone View Company published this stereoview card of a man spraying lead arsenate on potato plants on a truck farm in Princess Anne County. This poison killed potato bugs, which up to that time decimated, if not destroyed, the potato crop. A truck farmer who harvested 250 bushels of potatoes one year dug 3,200 bushels of potatoes the following year from the same parcel of land after he sprayed lead arsenate six times. This stereoview dates to about 1900. *Courtesy of the author.*

property were stored at the Archaeological Project Center at the College of William and Mary. Curtis Moyer, an anthropology lecturer at the college, was quoted in the April 10, 1989 *Virginian-Pilot*, speaking of the Ferry Farm site: "It's the most awe-inspiring collection from that period I've seen. It's got a little bit of everything. Normally, you'd have to go to many sites to acquire all this range of material," he said. He gave some examples of the curious items that would require further study, like sturgeon bones. "Our sturgeon don't run up the river anymore," he explained. Hunter and his colleagues pulled the bones out of the ground in August 1986, according to the report. Underfunded, the study of the artifacts stopped. But development of the Ferry Farm property moved forward. The house is today situated in the middle of the Old Donation Farm subdivision's one-and-a-half-acre open space. After the initial phase of development was completed, Old Donation Farm's homeowners association agreed to maintain a buffer of only fifteen feet around the house in exchange for the group's use of the house as a meeting place after restoration. Meanwhile, Ferry Farm sat neglected and isolated on its tiny patch of the subdivision.

More than ten years would pass after the archaeological dig that uncovered the farm's treasure-trove of colonial Princess Anne's past. With the house in dire need of restoration, a group of citizens jumped in and formed the Friends of the Ferry Plantation House. Through their hard work and lobbying for the property, it was deeded over to the City of Virginia Beach in June 1996; it remains a work in progress. "To me this is the most significant historical site in Virginia Beach," observed Councilwoman Barbara M. Henley, in the July 26, 1996 *Virginia Beach Beacon*. The councilwoman was one of the earliest to voice her support of the farmhouse's preservation. She remains a steadfast supporter today.

Nearly a quarter century before, Helen Crist hoped, like Reasor, that those who believed so fervently in historic preservation would do less talking and more acting to save the last bit of Fairfield and other treasured pieces of the city of Virginia Beach's past. "Maybe they will work harder," she wrote in 1972, "to spare them the same fate." There was even a threat just then to Peter Singleton I's Pleasant Hall. Reasor said at the time, "They're letting that go, too." But Pleasant Hall was spared and is today on the national and state historic registers. Sadly, that would not be the outcome for the little Fairfield house. Just before it came down, Crist speculated that there would be two kinds of people watching: misty-eyed onlookers asking themselves, "How in the world did it happen?" and others, seeing it go, who would say, "Good riddance. It's no loss; it was old anyway." The following month, the little Fairfield house was marked for demolition. When she called Reasor to find out what was happening,

Bucolic dairy farms like Fox Hall, shown here, are long gone from the modern Virginia Beach landscape. Located along the old Princess Anne Turnpike, Fox Hall was an important supplier of dairy products to Norfolk and its surrounding communities. Morris Stanley Secord was superintendent of the farm when Harry Mann took this picture sometime in 1914. *Courtesy of the author.*

he told her that a contract had been signed and that a builder would soon tear down the house. The regret that so many had after the house fell to a bulldozer was palpable. No doubt the generations of Walkes buried up on the ridge behind the house were equally disappointed. After all, they could not have imagined what might replace their elegant home and sprawling plantation.

A LITTLE TOWN NAMED
VIRGINIA BEACH

For a very long time, there was no Virginia Beach and no seaside resort on the Atlantic Ocean below Cape Henry. No one ever went there. Virginia's golden shore was a beautiful blank canvas, a resort in waiting with no name. The August 14, 1881 *Norfolk Virginian* called it the "watering place that is to be." Still, it had no name. But the report went on to inform readers that Norfolk entrepreneur and civil engineer Colonel Marshall Parks's development company was moving forward to make it "the most attractive resort along the Atlantic coast." The *Norfolk Virginian*'s reporter crafted a beautifully written, if inaccurate, description of the beach. This as yet unnamed beach would not have been "entirely free of debris, sea grass, shells, and pebbles." Debris, sea grass, shells and pebbles were strewn all over the beach, and in 1890 the resort's first streets were paved with seashells. "When we drove down the beach," continued the writer, "the wheels of the carriage hardly made an impression." Despite the article's utopian spin, we do learn that two and a half miles away the Lynnhaven River had already become famous for "the very best of oysters."

The story was written to capture the public's imagination; it mentions other place names that ring more familiar, Fort Monroe and Hampton Roads, as well as "the beautiful maritime scenery" for which the region was already known. But still no mention of "Virginia Beach." No one had given it a name, the reporter wrote. "As yet no name [has been] given to the place. The company is anxious to have a name that will be fully

Virginia Beach's Cottage Line was a mix of privately and commercially owned cottages that lent character and distinction to the seashore they fronted. Harry C. Mann took this picture about 1910; it shows the wooden boardwalk that was first built in 1888. The Arlington Hotel is farthest away, located just south of 13th Street and marked by the American flag flying out front. The Arlington was one of the town's earliest hotels but became a particularly important one after the Princess Anne Hotel burned to the ground on June 10, 1907. The Baptist Church of Virginia bought the Arlington in the 1910s and converted it to a summer retreat. Part of the Atkinson Cottage is in the picture, extreme left, and Burton Cottage is in full view, left foreground. Identifiable cottages beyond Burton include Carrington Cottage, also known as the Mount Vernon; Garwood Cottage, later called the Atlantic Cottage, and the DeWitt Cottage. Beyond DeWitt was the Glennan Cottage, Arlington Hotel, Booth Cottage, Ferebee Cottage and the Raleigh Bar. The windmill on the left pumped water for the Holland residence and nearby cottages. Only the DeWitt Cottage stands today. The Flume, a device that channeled salt water into Lake Holly for mosquito control, is on the right, jutting into the ocean. *Courtesy of the author.*

distinctive, and offer a prize for a name. The party who suggests a name and is accepted by the company will get the prize. This offer includes the ladies." There is no record of the contest nor any of the names that might have been suggested.

The first recorded use of the name "Virginia Beach" did not occur until the following year, on January 14, 1882, when the Virginia

The Princess Anne Hotel was built at 14th Street and Atlantic Avenue in 1884 as the Virginia Beach Hotel, a modest resort destination, until a railroad and development company reorganization in 1887 brought major improvements and a new name to the old hotel. Within a year, the name "Princess Anne" was known far and wide as the place to stay on Virginia's golden shore. When renovations were complete, the hotel had a new fourth floor and, as shown here, a glass-enclosed veranda to accommodate off-season visitors. This photograph was taken between 1900 and 1905. The hotel burned to the ground on June 10, 1907. *Courtesy of the Detroit Publishing Company Photograph Collection, Library of Congress, Prints and Photographs Collection.*

General Assembly approved the reorganization of Parks's Norfolk and Sewell's Point Railroad to the Norfolk and Virginia Beach Railroad and Improvement Company. The company's charter would be voided if it failed to complete a rail line to Virginia Beach in five years. Parks had his railroad operational the next year.

Marshall Ott Parks was born November 8, 1820, at Old Point Comfort, where his father, Marshall Parks, managed the Hygeia Hotel. His mother was Norfolk-born Martha Sweeney Frances Sayer Boush. Parks's rise in the world of business was meteoric between 1850 and 1860, when he ascended from Hygeia Hotel clerk to president of the Albemarle and Chesapeake Canal. He was still head of the canal company in 1870, but in the years to come (and up to the time of his death on June 12, 1900) Parks poured his effort into developing Virginia Beach into a resort destination like no other. Even after his company foreclosed, he continued to be one of its biggest boosters. Before he established the Norfolk and Virginia Beach Railroad and Improvement Company, Parks stood up the Seaside Hotel and Land Company in 1880. Between 1880 and 1882, his land company negotiated the purchase of eleven farms from Princess Anne County landowners that totaled 1,350 acres that ran like a ribbon five miles parallel to the Atlantic Ocean. In 1882, the Norfolk and Virginia Beach Railroad and Improvement Company took control of Parks's hotel and land company and all of its holdings.

Parks's vision for this ribbony strip of beach began to take shape more quickly after he broke ground at Broad Creek in January 1883 for his railroad's eighteen-mile track to the beach. The first trip by rail to the

The Norwegian bark *Dictator* was bound from Pensacola, Florida, to West Bartlepool, England, with a full load of lumber when it encountered significant weather off the Atlantic Coast. The ship's master, Captain Jorgen Martinius Jorgensen, made the decision to bring the *Dictator* into Norfolk to make repairs. The bark had just passed the Princess Anne Hotel and reached about 40th Street when it grounded and started breaking apart. Jorgensen's wife and infant son were drowned. Those who perished, including Jorgensen's wife and child, are buried in Norfolk's Elmwood Cemetery. The *Dictator*'s figurehead was brought to shore and erected in memorial in front of the hotel. Several decades later, in 1962, the wooden figurehead was replaced with a bronze one. This undivided-back postcard, showing the *Dictator* figurehead, was mailed on May 3, 1906. *Courtesy of the author.*

Members of the Tidewater Pleasure Club, a men's social group, met regularly at Cape Henry at the Hancock Cottage, an accommodation that was more shack than cottage, located over the dune and not far from William O'Keefe's casino. Club members were photographed at an oyster roast in November 1896; oysters on the half shell and bowls of oyster stew were being served all around. Hancock family members belonged to the Tidewater Pleasure Club and are identifiable in additional pictures at Cape Henry, with the club and at the cottage. *Courtesy of the author.*

This photograph, dated March 7, 1896, and taken during the winter season along Virginia Beach's Cottage Line, includes (left to right) Thomas Turner, Cornelia Tucker, Isaac Talbot Walke and Jenny Drewry. Despite the cold, the town's budding oceanfront provided social gatherings and plenty of entertainment that drew year-round visitors from nearby Norfolk for evening sojourns and extended weekend stays. *Courtesy of the Sargeant Memorial Room, Norfolk Public Library.*

Marshall Parks and his Princess Anne Hotel investors started the Norfolk and Virginia Beach Railroad and Improvement Company to move visitors from Norfolk to the Oceanfront. The first train, operated on a narrow-gauge track, left downtown Norfolk on July 16, 1883, bound for Virginia Beach. The train station at 17th Street and Pacific Avenue became the primary stop for hotel passengers. The railroad became the Norfolk and Southern in 1900, and the track was pushed out to Cape Henry. The 17th Street Station, photographed by Harry Mann circa 1910 and turned into a postcard, was open long after excursion trains delivered passengers to the Oceanfront; it served as a depot for the Virginia Beach Railbus Company and also as a bus station. The Norfolk and Southern train pulling up to the station on this postcard arrived on track that is today Pacific Avenue. *Courtesy of the author.*

Oceanfront was made on July 16, 1883, when Parks, company officers and invited guests made the winding trip through rural Princess Anne County to their final destination, a gracious pavilion being erected at the end of the line, presumably the Virginia Beach Club House. Lumber used to build everything from the pavilion to picnic tables came from nearby stands of pine. The Norfolk to Virginia Beach Railroad delivered 6,565 people to the beach between July 28 and September 30, 1883. Parks's patrons were happy enough, satisfied with opportunities to dance, picnic and play in the surf. But Parks wanted to offer the same seaside amenities that were already becoming popular at the New Jersey shore, most of them associated with improved health and recreation.

The following year, in 1884, the Seaside Hotel and Land Company built the Virginia Beach Hotel at 14th Street and Atlantic Avenue. This first beach hotel had sweeping views of the ocean from generously appointed

Norfolk and Southern Railroad built Seaside Park on three full blocks from 30th to 33rd Streets; it was opened in 1906 as the ultimate oceanfront resort for the railroad's excursion cars that dropped passengers at the park's station. Additional buildings and amusements, including a casino, were added to the park. Seaside Park's bathhouses, located beneath the picnic pavilion on the right, were state of the art for the period. This postcard was used in 1914. *Courtesy of the author.*

verandas. But three years after its construction, the hotel and railroad were sold in foreclosure, only to be reformed under a plan devised by Pennsylvania corporate lawyer Charles William Mackey, who came to the Virginia shore with a reputation as "a positive genius for organization." Virginia Beach needed everything he had to offer. In whole or in part during the course of Mackey's career, he organized a hundred or more corporations with aggregate capital nearing $150 million, including more than twenty railroad companies, six gas companies, sixty-seven manufacturing companies, eight to ten banks, three companies for the reduction of ores and several coal mining and quarrying companies. One of those railroads was Parks's Norfolk and Virginia Beach Railroad, which under Mackey's management established at Virginia Beach "a beautiful summer and winter resort."

The man credited with getting the Virginia Beach resort back on track has received little recognition for his hard work. Mackey was born on November 19, 1842, in Pennsylvania's Allegheny Valley. At the early age

The Groves Bath House, situated south of Seaside Park, had the first saltwater pool at Virginia Beach. Harry Mann took this picture about 1908. The bathhouse was developed by James Sundy Groves, owner and president of the Virginia Beach Land Development Company, a syndicate that owned much of what was early Virginia Beach. Groves was a Fayetteville, North Carolina native who married the former Lillie Ball Edwards in Lincoln County, Georgia, in the spring of 1881; he soon became a wealthy real estate broker and commercial merchant, with deep pockets and important contacts up and down the East Coast. While he worked largely from Alexandria, Virginia, and Washington, D.C., Groves kept an office in Norfolk, from which he ran his Virginia Beach investment. He also continued to deal produce from the city's Roanoke Square, a trade he learned as a fruit dealer in his youth. Groves first built a part-time residence at the corner of 25th Street and the Oceanfront in 1890 for his family's recreation; he later moved them into the stone cottage at 24th Street after the house was finished in 1906. Lillie Groves gave up the house after her husband died on February 16, 1916, at age fifty-seven at his home in Washington. *Courtesy of the author.*

of eighteen, he started his law studies. When the Civil War broke out, he was commissioned a first lieutenant in the Tenth Pennsylvania Reserve Volunteers. While his service has been described in official records as "conspicuously useful and meritorious," the backstory of his Civil War experience proved the true measure of his character; it is not a story readily found in Mackey's biographies. The Tenth Pennsylvania Volunteers, also known as the Thirty-ninth Infantry Regiment Pennsylvania, fought at

Norfolk architect and contractor James N.W. Porter filed a patent application for the self-latching automatic railway switch on January 13, 1908; it was approved by the United States Patent Office on July 13, 1909. Porter's switch was especially designed for use on electric or other tramway lines. His device was tested on the Virginia Beach Direct, shown here on April 29, 1909, leaving downtown Norfolk via City Hall Avenue; the Monticello Hotel is on the right. *Courtesy of the author.*

nearly all major battles in Virginia and Maryland, including the Battle of Fredericksburg, Virginia, after which he was court-martialed and convicted of violation of the Fifty-second Article of War, accused of abandoning his company and regiment while they were preparing to move to the front to engage the enemy on or about December 13, 1862. He pleaded "not guilty."

What happened at Fredericksburg was later determined to be beyond Charles Mackey's control. His division, led by Major General George Gordon Meade, became detached from the Union main force and was unsupported when it moved forward down the Richmond road. Overwhelmed, Meade's men broke and fled in disorder, leaving a large number of dead and wounded on the field and several hundred prisoners in

James Porter had a photographer waiting for the Virginia Beach Direct at its oceanfront destination; the station building in the background advertises "Virginia Beach—Cape Henry—Lynnhaven." The picture was also taken on April 29, 1909, the day Porter chose to test his self-latching automatic railway switch, and is one of a series of photographs of his invention and the test taken at that time. *Courtesy of the author.*

Galilee Protestant Episcopal by the Sea Chapel was a little piece of civilization at the Oceanfront. Reverend Beverly Dandridge Tucker held the first church services at Virginia Beach in his cottage but eventually raised enough money to build this interdenominational church. Galilee eventually became solely Episcopal. The chapel shown here was completed in 1891 at 17th Street on cottage row. This picture of the chapel was published on a postcard postmarked November 2, 1911. *Courtesy of the author.*

The monoplane *Virginia I* was photographed at Virginia Beach in August 1910. The aircraft shown here shares many similarities with Hungarian engineer Alexander L. Pfitzner's monoplane, built at Glenn Hammond Curtiss's Hammondsport factory and introduced in January 1910: it is a pusher and set on four wheels. These shared traits were atypical of monoplanes of this period, most of them being built in the tractor configuration in which the engine is mounted with the propeller facing forward so that the aircraft is pulled through the air as opposed to pushed. There are no specifics as to who designed and built the monoplane pictured. The photograph was taken just down the beach from the Princess Anne Hotel. *Courtesy of the Library of Congress, Prints and Photographs Division.*

Harry C. Mann took this picture of the beach entrance from Seaside Park's bathhouses about 1910. Behind the flag is a sign advertising the Slide for Life, billed as a thrilling and exciting ride. The slide was rigged with a harness that carried bathers down a long wire into the surf; it cost just a nickel for one ride and a quarter for six. *Courtesy of the author.*

Ocean Park, located just west of the Lynnhaven Inlet, was photographed by Harry Mann about 1910; the end of a new boardwalk is present but incomplete. Bathers got to Ocean Park via a stop on the electric rail line. The Ocean Park Casino opened here in 1926, many years after Mann took this picture, but three years later, half of it was destroyed by fire. Though the casino was rebuilt, Mother Nature wasn't done with this disaster-plagued park. Gale-force winds whipped through the park in January 1933 and did substantive damage; the now famous hurricane that came through Hampton Roads in August 1933 completely destroyed it. *Courtesy of the author.*

the hands of advancing Confederate forces. Mackey was, indeed, not guilty, and his record quickly expunged of the court-martial. He was promoted to captain and continued to serve through Gettysburg in June 1863.

After he was discharged from the army on June 27, 1863, Mackey accepted the appointment of special agent of the treasury from Secretary of the Treasury Salmon Portland Chase and was assigned to the Eastern District of Maryland, Virginia and North Carolina. He served in this role until August 1, 1865, when he tendered his resignation and returned to practicing law and fixing broken companies.

Under Mackey's direction, the Virginia Beach Hotel was expanded by the railroad from 50 to 139 rooms and took up two blocks from 14th to 16th Streets, with a railroad stop at its front door. The hotel's guest list was a who's who of politicians, captains of industry and American inventors: Presidents of the United States Benjamin Harrison and Grover Cleveland, William Jennings Bryan, Robert Green Ingersoll, Samuel Gompers, Cornelius Vanderbilt, Cyrus West Field and Alexander Graham Bell among others.

Four years after it was opened, the hotel's name was changed to the Princess Anne, and it was put under the management of New York hotelier Simeon E. Crittenden. Soon after Crittenden took over, the Princess Anne became one of the premier vacation destinations on the East Coast, the star attraction of newly minted Virginia Beach. North and south of the Princess Anne beach property, owners built impressive seaside cottages with wide porches and big windows to take advantage of the ocean air. Back in those days, swimming was done in the early morning and late afternoon to avoid sunburn. Young ladies, most of them from out of town, made the train trip to Norfolk dressed

Harry Mann was standing just above 14th Street looking south at the first Virginia Beach boardwalk when he took this photograph, which he could not have taken before June 10, 1907, when the Princess Anne Hotel burned to the ground. The Raleigh Bar, prominently advertised on a boardwalk sign, was established after the hotel fire. The bar's owners salvaged the bar from the Princess Anne's rathskeller. Mann made his photograph into this postcard, which was mailed on July 25, 1911. *Courtesy of the author.*

William O'Keefe, proprietor of the wildly popular Cape Henry Casino, had the inn shown here built on the southeast corner of 16th Street and Atlantic Avenue in 1902; he also lived there. To locals and out-of-town visitors, it was known as O'Keefe's Inn. But as the resort grew in size and popularity, O'Keefe jacked up the inn, moved it across the street to the oceanfront and renamed it Courtney Terrace, and Henry Gillen photographed it on May 3, 1928. After several additions, all of which are present in this picture, the inn was complete. O'Keefe died on July 1, 1937, and Courtney Terrace was demolished in 1959. *Courtesy of the author.*

in their finest batiste and lace, or sometimes organdie, as well as wide-brimmed hats and parasols. They were the cream of society, from Richmond, Lynchburg and Staunton to Washington, D.C., Boston and New York.

Virginia Beach's future first mayor, Bernard Peabody Holland, was barely eighteen when he came to the Virginia shore in 1885. Land was selling for twenty-five cents per acre, and opportunity was everywhere. He rented bicycles to the Princess Anne's visitors. When interviewed by Kay Doughtie Sewell in March 1956, the eighty-nine-year-old Fluvanna native recalled fondly that the Barrymore children, Ethel, John and Lionel, used to love to ride the bicycles around and around the pavilion. They were attractive, lively children. Another visitor who stuck in his

The cornerstone of the First Baptist Church of Virginia Beach was laid on April 21, 1908, at the corner of 17th Street and Arctic Avenue; this picture of the church was made into a postcard dated 1909, just after construction was completed. *Courtesy of the author.*

mind was not nearly as attractive. He had "a big, fat face, a big nose, and side whiskers. He used to spend a lot of time on the beach in front of the hotel, with his pant legs rolled up, flying kites. He was always experimenting," Holland remembered, "always preoccupied." The man was Alexander Graham Bell. Bell and his family were regular visitors to the Princess Anne, but sometimes he came alone. During a solo visit in December 1901, he scouted a location for his tetrahedral kite research but found the area from Virginia Beach up to Cape Henry unsuitable because of the telegraph wires and tall pines that might interfere with landing the kite.

Holland had been living and working at Virginia Beach for ten years when he took a wife and built her a house on a strip of land that ran from the shore to Lake Holly at 12th Street. Upstairs, on the third floor, he located a wireless telegraph station. From his telegraph room, Holland sent and received all of the news of happenings from the shore. He eventually served two noncontiguous terms as the town's mayor, the first after the resort was incorporated in March 1906 and which lasted for two years, and the second from 1913 to 1916. Fifty

The State Rifle Range, also later called the State Military Reservation, was established on a 350-acre parcel just south of the resort town of Virginia Beach that James Groves first offered to the commonwealth in June 1908. The first parcel was acquired from Groves in 1911, and initial construction was completed in November 1912. Norfolk and Southern Railroad ran a spur to the rifle range to facilitate the movement of troops to the reservation. A large contingency of the Virginia National Guard's First Brigade arrived by train there in July 1913 to engage in their summer camp and training. The men of the First Brigade named their tent city Camp H.M. Dickson, shown in this rare photograph taken over the period between July 6 and 13, 1913. *Courtesy of the author.*

years later, he could still tell detailed stories of people he had met and the events that had unfolded.

"All the best people in Virginia used to come to the Beach," he told Sewell, "and the finest families in Norfolk. Then there were all these notables." Back then, famous faces were the rule, not the exception. As she spoke to Holland, Sewell looked over his shoulder, admiring the weathered but noble carved lion's head; it came from the wreckage of the fated Norwegian bark *Dictator* that ran aground off the hotel on March 27, 1891. Holland's own experience with the shipwreck had a happier ending. He had been ill for several days in his room on the hotel's third floor. One night, he got up about nine o'clock, and as he passed in front of the window, he looked out toward the beach. There, backlit by a bright moon, he thought he saw the majestic figure of a woman looking out to sea. What he saw, instead, was the figurehead of the *Dictator*, which had been first spotted by Emily Randall Gregory, a visitor from Cooperstown, New York. She notified hotel management, and with the help of several strong men, the figurehead was pulled to shore and stood up in the sand. Four years later, the young woman who found it became his wife.

Emily Gregory came from a wealthy family. Granddaughter Ann Francis Holland called her grandparents "the odd couple." Her grandmother, she wrote later, hated her life in Cooperstown, except for the opera, which she loved; the Gregorys had box seats at New York's old Metropolitan Opera. "She particularly loved Wagner." Her grandmother otherwise found her life there "boring and superficial. She used to say of it: 'We sat and sat and sat, and then we sat some more. The only work these ladies ever did,' she opined, 'was needlework, which as you know, came in handy later on and a bit of baking of special cakes and pies.' She

Camp H.M. Dickson was flooded by a heavy rain storm on July 10, 1913, the date this exceptionally rare view of the men of the First Brigade was photographed at the State Rifle Range. *Courtesy of the author.*

was also very well read, an intellectual and a gifted musician; [she] played the piano, violin, viola and sang."

During one of the winter trips of Emily's parents, David Henderson and Emily Weld Randall Gregory, to Saint Augustine, Florida, they stopped at the Princess Anne Hotel, and there she met and fell in love with Bernard Holland; he fell immediately in love with her as well. Some called it love at first sight. "She was rich, intellectual and fat," recalled Ann Holland. "He was slim, dapper and unintellectual, though far from unintelligent. Her parents persuaded them to wait a couple of years. They were married in 1895 in Cooperstown, where her parents had a summer home they called Sunnyside."

Renting bicycles and being mayor were not the bookends of Holland's career. He was superintendent of the Norfolk, Virginia Beach and Southern Railroad and also an officer of the Princess Anne Hotel, where he lived until he built the first of two cottages for Emily, the second also located on 12th Street but one block inland from the first; Holland called the residence Ozone. He was also a shrewd real estate developer and was well connected. In addition to the land on which he built his first cottage in 1895, he also bought property at Birdneck Point and Back Bay. His connections with the hotel's distinguished roster of guests afforded friendship and business opportunities. Among the captains of industry and American politics he knew well were farm equipment manufacturers the McCormick family and United States senator James Gillespie Blaine from Maine, whose oldest son, Emmons Blaine, eventually married the McCormicks' eldest daughter.

In the middle of his second term as mayor, Bernard Holland became extremely ill, and in 1916 he resigned from the railroad. In the years to come, he almost died several times. No one knew what caused his sickness until Emily took him back to New York, where her family owned a hospital room. There, according to Ann Holland, he was diagnosed with an inoperable inflammation of the secum, the flap that allows food into the stomach. From Ann Holland, we know that Bernard and Emily came back to Virginia Beach, where she took over support of the family. "[She] took in boarders," she wrote, "and rented out the house. She sent the children to Sunnyside and lived in the attic while summer renters lived downstairs. She opened The Variety Shop which had a lending library, yarn goods, etc. She did knitting and sewing for people. She sold

This 1915 photograph shows the Sam Simmons Orchestra playing Seaside Park's famous Peacock Ballroom, located in one of the park's original pavilions; Sam Simmons is at the piano. Orchestras of national reputation started coming to the Peacock in the late 1910s and 1920s, and by the 1930s the big-band sound made its debut. Tommy Dorsey played the Peacock for the first time in 1936; he charged ten cents for one dance or three for a quarter. *Courtesy of the author.*

a valuable piece of jewelry and probably some other things." This is how she managed to send the couple's three oldest boys to the University of Virginia. Their only daughter, Cornelia, was given teaching lessons at the shore. She never got a formal education. But after five years passed, Emily cured her husband with a change of diet.

All that Emily Holland did to take care of her family, opined granddaughter Ann, came at a high price, and Cornelia paid it. She was no more than a child when her mother put her in charge of younger brother David and all of the household chores. At that time, it was not unusual for the eldest or only daughter to assume her mother's role in the house. "Grandma always regretted sacrificing Nini [Cornelia's family nickname]. It was one of the last things she said before she died." Despite the trials of her early life, Cornelia would become as beloved to the Virginia Beach community as her mother and father had been. But

Emily never really got over what she did to her only daughter. "[Though] it was not unusual in those days for the eldest or only daughter to take over the mother role, Grandma realized that it was a tragedy. We all know that Nini was very much in love with a young man and [had been] forbidden to marry him. They bought her off with a trip to Europe and the promise of the property." Even after her husband recovered, Emily kept her store. Bernard Holland was never again as successful as he had been before his illness. He bought a general store, and they lived out their lives at Ozone. She died in 1949, and he died in January 1960 at the age of ninety-three.

It is fortunate for all of us that Bernard Holland filled in the blanks of early Virginia Beach history before his death. How else would we know today how Back Bay came into its own or what was going on down at the Cape Henry weather station or what the first town council was like? We

Before it became Albemarle Hall in 1919, this hostelry was the beach residence of North Carolina native and Norfolk seed merchant James C. Tait and his family and was known as Marguerite Cottage, named for one his daughters, born in January 1899 and whose birth coincided with the period during which the family took up part-time residence there. James Tait died on a trip to the Biltmore in Asheville, North Carolina, on August 29, 1919, and the cottage was sold to another North Carolina native, John Stanley Smith, and his wife, the former Annie Shaw. Before buying the Marguerite from Tait's widow, Smith was employed as a government purchasing agent. The Smith family owned and operated Albemarle Hall as a hotel for half a century. *Courtesy of the author.*

This rare penny postcard of the Greenlee (center), an early hunting club, and Life-Saving Station No. 2 at 24ᵗʰ Street and the Oceanfront (left), was mailed on September 13, 1920, although the picture predates the 1906 construction of a stone cottage to the right of the Greenlee that later served as a part-time residence for the James S. Groves and James C. Tait families before Norfolk businessman Garrett Smith turned it into the new Princess Anne Hotel in 1922. The station was opened in 1903 to replace its aged 1878 predecessor, which was relocated a block inland and out of view in this picture, and the Greenlee later became the Breakers Hotel. *Courtesy of the author.*

would know little of it had it not been for his sharp memory and quick wit. Holland was an avid duck hunter. He told Kay Sewell that Marshall Parks spent his last years trying to get the federal government to construct a canal from the Lynnhaven River to Back Bay to create an inland waterway system. Currituck Inlet already drew enough saltwater into Currituck Sound and Back Bay to raise the salinity of the bay. "There were plenty of oysters in there [the bay] at the time; the shells are still there to show for it," he observed. "But after the inlet was closed, the waters in Back Bay became fresh, and soon there was a tremendous crop of luscious duck grasses. Wildfowl came down in hordes. For over one hundred years Back Bay has been one of the most used duck hunting grounds in the country."

Norfolk market gunners hunted the thousands of canvasbacks and redheads that flew into Back Bay and shipped their kill to buyers in the North. "The hunters," Holland recalled in some detail, "used very large guns. Some of the birds were shot from swivels on boats. Some of the

The western side of Lynnhaven Inlet included the Lynnhaven Hotel (shown here on the left). The bathhouse is center, and the Shell House, which offered shells and other souvenirs for sale, is on the right, at the water's edge. Out of view is the quick slide into the river. The John A. Lesner Bridge, opened in 1928, is not visible but is on the right behind the Shell House. The picture dates to 1924. All of the motorcycles are Harley-Davidsons, from the 1918 18-J with sidecar to the newest 1924 model; the riders started their ride at Raymond C. Almond's new Harley-Davidson dealership at Norfolk's 726 Granby Street. Almond was on the ride with them with his partner, Harry Hunt Garrett. A Ford Model T is to the far left. *Courtesy of Raymond C. Almond Jr.*

market gunners lived on little houseboats built low, on logs, and anchored out in the bay near [large concentrations of the duck]." Even President Harrison liked to hunt on Back Bay. No one knew quite how much until the consummate Republican got an invitation to hunt duck he couldn't refuse: "I remember when Judge [William Nathaniel] Portlock and several local politicians came and invited Harrison to go ducking with them. [This] meant driving a big old wagon, bigger than a buckboard, over twenty miles of the roughest Princess Anne [County] roads—just to go ducking with Democrats. I tell you, it would take Back Bay to make a Republican ignore politics and go off hunting with his opponents."

As a telegraph operator, Holland supported the weather station at Cape Henry, which covered a wide swath of the coast from Virginia Beach to Cape Hatteras. After a big storm, weather station personnel would have to leave the bureau building, repair poles and restring the wire. "I'd help out," said Holland. "I'd take the messages and send them on to

Raymond C. Almond, on the right, is shown at Lynnhaven Inlet in front of the little resort that included the Lynnhaven Hotel, out of view to the far left; the Shell House is behind them. The Harley-Davidsons are 1925 JDs, the first year Harley-Davidson introduced the teardrop-shaped gas tank. The year of the photo would be the summer of 1928. The Lesner Bridge, a draw span, is complete and to the right of Almond in the photograph. *Courtesy of Raymond C. Almond Jr.*

the weather bureau in Norfolk, and they'd send them on to Washington. Those signals had precedence over everything; when they came in, everything else had to stop." But one day, he got an urgent telegram from the Norfolk Western Union office. The hotel manager wanted to know if he knew the *Norfolk Virginian* managing editor Michael Glennan and, if so, where he had gone. Holland ran out the door and down to the beach, sure that he had last seen him down there with his son, Keville. The Glennans were out on the sand. "I was running. What do you think was the news I had to bring? That the *Norfolk Virginian* newspaper building was burning down. Hadn't been built very long, either."

Holland's leadership of the first Virginia Beach Town Council was one of the most important contributions that he would make to the budding resort. He was ably assisted by a handpicked group of men, all them vested in some way to the community: Irish-born capitalist Daniel Stormont; Cape Henry Casino owner William John O'Keefe; James Sundy Groves, owner and president of the Virginia Beach Land Development Company; William J. Wright, who became town mayor from September 6, 1910, to

January 21, 1913, and headed the first commission to select the route of the Norfolk–Virginia Beach highway; Amos Johnston Ackiss, an attorney; and painting contractor John P. Jones. The first meeting of the council occurred at the Princess Anne Hotel on March 15, 1906. There, the members accepted the town charter, posted a notice to recruit a town sergeant, named a committee to establish rules of order and dissolved the incorporation committee that had secured the charter. The town council continued to hold its meetings at the hotel, which had also been sold that year to Groves's development company, quartered in offices off the hotel lobby. But his ownership of the grand dame of the shore was short-lived.

On the morning of June 10, 1907, the Princess Anne Hotel caught fire and burned to the ground. The fire that destroyed the hotel started in the kitchen, supposedly from a defective flue, and within two hours it had engulfed the hotel, the Norfolk and Southern Railroad depot, the bowling alley, a hotel laundry, the engine house, the office of the Virginia Beach Development Company and all of the boardwalk in front of the hotel. There were 110 guests and employees in the hotel. All were alerted to the fire by a young sergeant of the Richmond Light Artillery Blues, Herman Carl Boschen, who was on his way to the train station when he spotted the flames. He rushed into the hotel to alert guests and staff but was eventually overcome by smoke and had to be carried from the building. Two deaths were initially reported: Emma Clark, an African American chambermaid, and John Eaton, a steward. Insurance did not cover the entire loss. The hotel safe, containing heavy receipts and thousands of dollars worth of guest valuables, was not locked, and all contents were lost. There were unconfirmed reports that an unnamed guest and friend of the hotel's manager was also missing. Later that day, Manager Mitchell tried to kill himself by jumping into the ocean. Twenty years would pass before a hotel as grand and important as the Princess Anne was built at Virginia Beach.

Transportation to the Oceanfront had vastly improved before the hotel fire. Though it was competition for the Norfolk Southern, the Chesapeake Transit Company started construction on its own rail line to Virginia Beach through Cape Henry in 1901. At that time, the Norfolk Southern Railway stopped at a point near what is today 16th Street. When Norfolk Southern saw that Chesapeake Transit's line came down from the north, Norfolk

The trip over Lynnhaven Inlet was made easier for this group of Harley-Davidson riders after Shore Drive was opened in 1928 in conjunction with the John A. Lesner Bridge and to relieve traffic on Virginia Beach Boulevard. This photograph, taken about 1928, includes not only the Harley-Davidson group but also car traffic coming up behind the men standing partly in the road. Shore Drive became a busy road almost immediately after it opened; whenever the draw span was opened for boat traffic, Shore Drive became a temporary parking lot. The 1928 span was replaced three decades later with a bridge that no longer required a draw span to allow boats to pass. *Courtesy of Raymond C. Almond Jr.*

Southern pushed its track up to Pacific Avenue and to about 25th Street and then across to the Oceanfront to cut off the new line. Chesapeake Transit superintendent George Lewis could play that game, too. He hid railroad ties and rails where the Cavalier Hotel now stands, and in the cover of darkness he took a work crew, laid a line across the Norfolk Southern track and continued down the shore near the Princess Anne Hotel. Chesapeake Transit's rail service was open for service in 1903. The Norfolk Southern was savvy to what Lewis had done. Only a short time passed before the Norfolk Southern countered and ran a parallel track from Virginia Beach to Cape Henry. After the two railroads merged as the Norfolk and Southern, the company took up the parallel track. The Norfolk and Southern ran a successful electric loop from Norfolk to Cape Henry to Virginia Beach and then back to Norfolk again.

Long before the Pennsylvania Railroad acquired 1,800 acres to build a terminal, and before the United States Navy later developed the largest amphibious base in the world there, Little Creek was a fishing ground well documented to at least the late eighteenth century and probably far longer. In its pre-navy period, the area was a pleasure boat haven. This picture of Little Creek was taken in 1920, six years before the Pennsylvania Railroad acquired its first parcel of land. More development soon followed. Little Creek, located twelve miles northeast of Norfolk off what was then the Ocean View–Virginia Beach scenic highway, became an important training ground for the navy's amphibious force starting in April 1942, when the navy got its toehold on a waterlogged bean field in the Whitehurst farm area. *Courtesy of the author.*

The Norfolk and Southern established the original Seaside Park in 1906. Stretched between 30th and 33rd Streets, Seaside Park was the ultimate beach resort; it had it all. Later, on June 1, 1912, a casino was added inside Seaside Park. The railroad ran dancing cars to which they gave snappy names like the "One-Step Special" and "Two-Step Express." Boarding the train at Norfolk's Monticello Avenue, patrons rode the train to make the Oceanfront ballrooms and music halls to dance the two-step and turkey trot to old tunes like "O! You Beautiful Doll" and "Alexander's Ragtime Band." The last train didn't leave the casino until eleven o'clock in the evening. During the Roaring Twenties, the waltz

Virginia governor Harry Flood Byrd, speaking from a podium behind the pine boughs on the right, addressed the pilgrimage ceremony at Cape Henry on April 26, 1928. This annual event is held in remembrance of the first Virginians to set foot there on April 26, 1607. Up until 1928, the ceremony was held on top of the sand dune near the old Cape Henry lighthouse, but that year a natural amphitheater was dug out by the wind at the foot of the dune, so it was used instead. Fort Story soldiers built a platform for Byrd and other speakers and raised a tall cross made from Cape Henry pine in front of it. *Courtesy of the author.*

and two-step were replaced by the Charleston and the shag. By then the casino was no longer the only place to go. The Jarvis Dance Hall played host to bob-haired flappers and their Rudolph Valentino look-alike dates who danced the night away in a smoke-choked ballroom that shook with great music and laughter.

There is so much more than can be written about early Virginia Beach, but the limit of space precludes it. But picture a simpler time. When it began, there were just fourteen cottages and two hotels, the Princess Anne and a lesser establishment called the Ocean View. The cottages belonged to the true pioneers of the town of Virginia Beach. At least one of them was built from lumber that had washed ashore from shipwrecks;

the cottage belonged to the family of James Allen. But the cottages are all gone now, save one: the 1895 Holland home bought by Cornelius deWitt in 1909 and renamed Wittenzand, Dutch for "white sand."

As the Oceanfront moved into more modern times after World War I, it was apparent to a new generation of seaside investors that singular dependency on the railroad to move people back and forth would continue to limit growth on the shore. Virginia Beach needed modern roadways and bridges to facilitate the use of the automobile. After the three Laskin brothers—Jacob, Elmer and Louis—partnered with Louis Siegel and leased Seaside Park and Casino in 1925, they were quick to equate future success to the ability to move people to the beach by car. At their own expense they built the first Laskin Road, formerly 31st Street, and deeded it over to the commonwealth. Laskin Road was eventually broadened to a four-lane highway, but by then the park had disappeared from the surfside scene. A fire swept through its concession buildings in 1934, including its popular restaurant. None of it was ever replaced. The swimming pool was still there in 1940, but it was later filled in. The park's famous combination bathhouse and picnic pavilion was torn down in 1950. The only building that lasted longer was the casino, but another fire took it and all the rest in the early 1950s.

BETWEEN WAR AND PEACE

For two decades the Virginia Beach shore had been missing a grand hotel. But on the eve of the 1926 season, the cornerstone was about to be laid for a new luxury hotel that was going to be built seven stories high on the top of a dune in the Seapines section of the resort at the end of 42nd Street. But it did not have a name. The Norfolk newspapers ran a naming contest to make sure that when it did open the name on the birth certificate was the right one. After many submissions, the names were narrowed to the Algonquin, the Crystal, the Sea Pine, the Linkhorn and The Cavalier (with a capital "T" for emphasis). Two months before the cornerstone laying, on March 5, 1926, a name was publicly announced: The Cavalier. The May 26, 1926 afternoon edition of the Norfolk newspaper, reporting on the cornerstone ceremony, remarked that the event was not only symbolic of the resort's "coming of age" but also of the commonwealth's significant progress since the turn of the century. This was the birth of the hotel that would later become the undisputed "aristocrat of Virginia's seashore."

Thirteen months later, The Cavalier Hotel opened with 195 rooms, none of which was very large by today's standards. Virginia governor Harry Flood Byrd, in attendance for the hotel's April 7, 1927 debut, called it "the best resort hotel in America." The hotel soon became famous from one end of the East Coast to the other. By the time Frank Blackford wrote about it over four decades later in the June 27, 1971

Men of Company K, 1st Infantry, Virginia National Guard, were photographed at the State Military Reservation, Virginia Beach, Virginia, in 1929. The 1st Infantry was later redesignated the 176th Infantry. Of important note, this reservation was established at a time when Virginia Beach was a small town and Princess Anne County was a rural, sparsely populated place. Today, it is sandwiched between General Booth Boulevard to the west, Birdneck Road to the south, the Croatan neighborhood to the north and the Atlantic

Virginian-Pilot, he observed that the hotel was a sign of an America dramatically changed from the days when the hotel was first opened. "Today's guests," he wrote, "are not interested in big name bands or service in the grand, old style."

Through its long history, The Cavalier courted the rich and famous, just as its predecessor, the Princess Anne Hotel, had done before it. From presidents of the United States to captains of industry and entertainment, The Cavalier played host to them all, including Calvin Coolidge, Herbert Hoover, Harry Truman, Dwight Eisenhower, John Kennedy, Lyndon Johnson, Richard Nixon, Gerald Ford and Jimmy Carter and then Ambassador to China George Herbert Walker Bush, later the forty-third president. Then there were the rest, too many to name them all, but here are a few: iconic American author F. Scott Fitzgerald and his wife, Zelda; entertainers Judy Garland, Bette Davis, Jean Harlow, Betty Grable, Frank

Ocean to the east. Though the city of Virginia Beach has encroached upon the reservation via public, residential and commercial development, it continues to provide important training facilities not only to the Virginia National Guard and other state guard units but also to the Military Sealift Command and units of the armed services that periodically use the camp's facilities. *Courtesy of the author.*

Sinatra and Fatty Arbuckle; and Hank Ketchum, creator of the *Dennis the Menace* cartoon. In its glory days, Charles "Buddy" Rogers's band played, and in between sets he courted Mary Pickford, America's silver screen sweetheart and top box office draw. They were married from 1937 to 1979, when she died. But Rogers was just one of the big-band leaders to play The Cavalier. There were others, including Russ Carlyle, Sammy Kaye, Les Brown and his Band of Renown, Benny Goodman, Vaughn Moore, Cab Calloway, Harry James, Jimmy Dorsey, Woody Herman, Artie Shaw, Glenn Miller and Lawrence Welk. The hotel became one of the largest employers of bands in the United States.

While most of The Cavalier's guests were more taken by the view of the Atlantic Ocean from their room, Will Rogers was not. Coming down to breakfast one morning, he was heard to quip that "Harry K. Thaw killed the wrong architect." He was referring, of course, to New York architect and married man Stanford White, whom Thaw accused of

Historically used primarily to train the Virginia National Guard, exceptions were made during World War I and World War II when the State Rifle Range was leased to the armed services. The immediate need for a facility to train ship crews in nearby Norfolk prompted the commonwealth to lease the range to the United States Navy for the duration of World War I. In August 1917, the navy took over the facility, temporarily renaming it the United States Navy Rifle Range, Virginia Beach. The navy did not vacate the reservation until the summer of 1920. Twenty years later, in October 1940, the federal government renamed it Camp Pendleton. Today, it is called the State Military Reservation Camp Pendleton. This picture of the machine gun range dates to the World War I period. *Courtesy of the author.*

spoiling their shared mistress Evelyn Nesbit before he shot him to death on the roof of Madison Square Garden on June 25, 1906.

The Cavalier came to be in much the same way as all of the other hotels and amusements on the Oceanfront: Norfolk investors, the railroads and East Coast passenger shipping lines put up the money to build it. Most of the hotel's guests in the first years it was open arrived by train. The Cavalier Special took on passengers daily in the Midwest and delivered them at the hotel's doorstep. The Norfolk and Western's motto was "The Cavalier to The Cavalier." Even the walk to the hotel got a little bit easier. Back in 1926, construction began on a new concrete walk; it was finished the following year. After the concrete was poured for this walkway, the term "boardwalk" stuck. But it did not go far enough down the beach to reach The Cavalier. A consortium of beach property owners formed the Virginia Beach Walkway Corporation to extend the concrete walk from 35th Street up to 50th Street. The new portion of the boardwalk was christened and opened to the public on May 26, 1928.

A groundbreaking ceremony was held on May 9, 1926, for the seven-story Cavalier Hotel; it was opened thirteen months later. The hotel's opening was a weeklong celebration held over the week of April 4, 1927. Colonel Samuel L. Slover, president of the Cavalier Hotel Corporation, and Virginia governor Harry Flood Byrd presided over the Cavalier's inaugural banquet on April 7, a meal that included the ubiquitous Lynnhaven oyster. This photograph was taken shortly after the hotel was opened. *Courtesy of the author.*

Early on, The Cavalier was also called the "Cavalier on the Hill" for the massive sand dune that pushed it far above the rest of the resort strip; it was more than a bricks-and-mortar experience from day one. For decades the owners of the hotel also held the option to much of the land around it, including homes in Cavalier Shores. Before World War II, most patrons stayed for at least ten days if not longer and enjoyed activities in the hotel's entertainment rooms and outdoor sporting opportunities. The hotel opened the Cavalier Beach Club on Memorial Day 1929 to the music of the McFarland Twins, who had earlier been the saxophonists for the Fred Waring Orchestra. This hotel beach club became the undisputed model for all beach clubs that opened on the Virginia Beach Oceanfront.

Before the war, in 1935, Professional Golf Association Hall of Famer Sam Snead won the Virginia Open on the Cavalier Golf Course. By this time, the hotel was touted as Virginia Beach's largest industry. Without question, it employed more people and paid more taxes than anyone else on the Virginia shore.

World War II changed everything for The Cavalier. The federal government notified hotel management on October 3, 1942, that the hotel would be needed as a radar training school for the United States Navy. Nearly all of the hotel space was converted to this purpose. When the hotel was returned to its owners at the end of the war, manager Sidney Banks came back, too. Banks had managed The Cavalier since

Film star Alice Joyce and her husband, James B. Regan Jr., were guests at The Cavalier Hotel in 1928 and are shown here on the beach. She was best known for her film contributions during the silent era and enjoyed the adoration of many fans, who nicknamed her "the Madonna of the Screen." She appeared in eighty films, starting with *The Engineer's Sweetheart* in 1910 and ending with *The Green Goddess* in 1930. Born in Kansas City, Missouri, on October 1, 1890, she died on October 9, 1955. Though a popular and much-loved silent film star, Joyce's career did not carry over into talking pictures, and she was largely forgotten by the time of her death. Most of her early films did not survive. *Courtesy of the author.*

1930, but the job he had ahead of him to put back what the navy had taken away was monumental. Pullman had discontinued rail service to the hotel, and patronage had dropped through the floor. The automobile was the preferred mode of transportation. The Cavalier Jefferson Hotel Corporation that owned it just then, and of which Banks was president, decided to transfer the deed to the hotel and its surrounding property to two emerging corporations: Cavalier Hotel Corporation and Northwest Development Company. Banks had been president of the former, and Gene Dixon, a Dillwyn, Virginia industrialist and head of Kyanite Mining Corporation, became Banks's vice-president. Banks's company held title to the hotel, beach club, inn, lodge and garage, and Northwest

Congressman Melville Clyde Kelly, a Pennsylvania Republican, vacationed with his family at The Cavalier Hotel about 1929 and is shown here playing croquet with his daughters (left to right) Hilda, Mary Jane, Vida Clyde and Ruth. Kelly sponsored the Air Mail Act of 1925, also called the Kelly Act, which authorized the postmaster to award contracts for airmail service to commercial carriers, a move that further propped up the nation's fledgling commercial airline industry. After it passed, he was known as the father of airmail. By 1933, he had become the top Republican on the Post Office Committee. *Courtesy of the author.*

Richard Crane, owner of Westover plantation in Charles City County and a former diplomat, had already begun development of Birdneck Point when he was approached by The Cavalier Hotel's ownership to build a club for its patrons that featured a first-rate golf course and trapshooting. He agreed and donated the land to the hotel for that purpose. The Cavalier Country Club was under construction on Birdneck Point when Henry Gillen took this picture in June 1930; the club was completed soon after. Professional Golf Association legend Sam Snead won the Virginia Open on the Cavalier Country Club's course in 1935. Today the club is called the Cavalier Yacht and Country Club. *Courtesy of the author.*

had the rest, including the Cavalier Golf and Yacht Club, completed in 1930 as the Cavalier Country Club, and a three-hundred-foot strip of land that adjoined the hotel and extended from the Oceanfront back to Holly Road. Northwest leased its holdings to Cavalier. After Banks sold his interest in the hotel in Dixon in 1961, this made Dixon the sole owner.

A devastating fire damaged the hotel's fifth floor in May 1969. The hotel remained open while expensive repairs were made. Dixon organized a new group of investors, mostly local men, and named James Myron Renfrow as The Cavalier's new manager. Renfrow took the job knowing that his biggest task was to keep the hotel solvent at the peak of

Members of the Virginia Commission of Game and Inland Fisheries diverted from their statewide game survey to take part in an oyster roast held at the Cavalier Country Club on October 11, 1930. *Virginian-Pilot* photographer Charles Simpson Borjes, who also freelanced for civic organizations and clubs, took this picture of commission officers and members (left to right) Lewis Williamson Tyus, fiscal secretary, of Richmond; Beverley William Stras Jr., of Tazewell; Noble Davis Hart, secretary, of Richmond; Major Absalom Willis Robertson, chairman, of Lexington, who derived his rank from his World War I service; Richard Crane, of Westover and developer of Birdneck Point; Samuel Philip Goodloe, of Afton; and Carl Henry Nolting, of Louisa. Robertson was chairman of the state game commission from 1926 to 1932. The following year, in 1933, Robertson was elected as a Democrat to the United States House of Representatives, in which he served until 1946, when he resigned to accept a nomination for the United States Senate. He was elected that November to fill the senate seat left vacant by the death of Carter Glass; he was reelected in 1948, 1954 and 1960. *Courtesy of the author.*

the national recession. The economy just then would not let him succeed. By 1973, Dixon had opened The Cavalier Oceanfront, at which time the original Cavalier, renamed Cavalier on the Hill, was closed. The Cavalier Oceanfront was built eleven stories high and rises today 120 feet over the beach. A year after it was closed, Dixon held a public auction of all contents of the Cavalier on the Hill. "They had come to pick at the old

This unusual photograph was taken on the night of June 21, 1932, during the thirty-third annual tournament of the Virginia Trap Shooters Association held at Virginia Beach. This was believed to have been the first time that such a tournament was conducted at night. Luminous clay pigeons were used. *Courtesy of the author.*

lady's bones," wrote Bob Lipper in the December 15, 1974 *Virginian-Pilot*, as bargain hunters, memorabilia collectors, businessmen and secondhand furniture dealers picked through the priceless memorabilia, goods, furnishings and hotel equipment looking for a deal. "These people," observed Lipper, "walked through the lobby quietly, then drifted into the Cavalier Room, the Colonial Room, the Garden Porch to poke with a certain degree of reverence through the heirlooms of an age left behind when we discovered neon and the interstate highway." After it was empty, it stayed that way. The property on which it was built was not for sale.

"It made me sad when they closed it," observed Sidney Banks after The Cavalier was shuttered. "I think it's still the queen of the Beach." The Cavalier on the Hill would not be closed long. The community that had grown up with it and around it missed the aristocrat terribly, and it was reopened in 1976. This was a reprieve from obscurity that everyone was glad to see.

Going back to that day at The Cavalier auction is instructive. Auctioneer Maury Riganto told Lipper something that none of us should forget:

Iconic photographer Charles Clyde Ebbets took this photograph of four young women at the gate to the Cavalier Beach Club in July 1932. Ebbets worked throughout the Southeast during this period, covering sports and social seasons in Miami, Augusta and Virginia Beach, as well as in New York City. Ebbets's Virginia Beach images were part of a photographic essay he called "Where the Sea Meets the Shore." *Courtesy of the author.*

"The Cavalier *is* Virginia Beach." As he watched a continuous flow of The Cavalier's memories walk out the door, he pointed and said again, "That's the Beach. When you say The Cavalier, that's Virginia Beach." What happened to Cavalier on the Hill in 1973 signaled an ongoing change of fortune for many of America's finest old hotels and attractions after World War II. They had become the unwanted victims of culture and economy. Many of them were closed because the land on which they were built was more valuable turned into a shopping center. That the Cavalier on the Hill was able to come back stronger after its near-death experience was the exception, not the rule.

In retrospect, The Cavalier and the rest of the Oceanfront's old places were at dire risk by the mid-1950s, even if no one realized it yet. Along Atlantic Avenue and on streets running parallel from the Oceanfront, the

The Cavalier Beach Club was opened on Memorial Day 1929 to the sweet sounds of the McFarland Twins, who had been saxophonists for the Fred Waring Orchestra. There were no other beach clubs at the Oceanfront before the Cavalier Beach Club. For thirty years, the club was the biggest employer of big bands. Bing Crosby joined Paul Whiteman's orchestra in 1927 as a singer, and the same year Crosby partnered with Harris Barris to form the Rhythm Boys. The "boys" played the beach club in 1930, shortly before they disbanded. The Cavalier Beach Club held tea dances every afternoon; the one shown here was photographed in 1934. *Courtesy of the author.*

constant drone of construction equipment and the steady chorus of hammers signaled another new building going up. But they weren't just hotels. Sprinkled in between were theaters, nightclubs, restaurants, storefronts, a bowling alley and a skating rink, as well as a few public buildings. The Virginia Beach Theater at 25th Street and Atlantic Avenue, opened in July 1946, was the handiwork of William C. Crockett and David Pender, who owned two additional cinema houses at the Oceanfront. Down on 35th Street and Atlantic Avenue, a two-story building with storefronts on the first floor and eighteen apartments upstairs was being completed. At the northwest

Hollywood B-western actor Bill Cody (seated center) was released by Monogram Pictures after an eight-picture run, and in late 1932, when Charles Clyde Ebbets took this photograph of him, he worked for a traveling Wild West show as its star attraction. Cody, no relation to Buffalo Bill Cody, stayed with the show through 1933; he returned to making B-westerns with Aywon Pictures the following year. Ebbets took a series of photographs of Cody and members of his Wild West extravaganza at the base of the old Cape Henry lighthouse. *Courtesy of the author.*

corner of 19th Street and Atlantic Avenue, a branch of the National Bank of Commerce was coming up next to a host of other new establishments.

Popular Oceanfront mainstays made improvements to keep up. Seaside Park launched a round of refurbishment projects that added a new bathhouse, the largest in Virginia, and a new concession building to the boardwalk. This building boom prompted Russell A. McCoy Jr., supervising engineer for the Town of Virginia Beach, to observe that the rate of construction in 1946—one year—far exceeded the cumulative building made in the decades leading up to World War II. This amazing surge started with the building of the Bank of Virginia Beach in the spring of 1945, the war then being over in Europe.

Just as surely as a way of life was changing, so was a way of life enjoyed for centuries in Princess Anne County, where the population spiked dramatically between 1950 and 1956. County planners published the numbers: the 42,000 residents who lived there in 1950 had nearly doubled to 82,500. This was a 96 percent increase in the population, all of it attributable to what will be explained fully in the chapter to follow: uncontrolled growth. Down at the Oceanfront, the rush to develop open space had a great impact because there was less of it to work with; buildings would have to come down before new ones could go up. The character of the resort was being chipped away. Increased property values meant higher taxes.

"I have watched the opening of a tract of land between the southern border of Seashore State Park and the northern shore of Crystal Lake at Virginia Beach," wrote Louisa Venable Kyle in the November 11, 1956

Royal Ambassador camp participants posed for this picture in 1937 in front of the Baptist Lodge at what is now 84th Street. The Royal Ambassador organization is a Southern Baptist mission education program for boys in grades first through sixth, first established in 1908. After camping became a very important part of Royal Ambassador work, the first camp was held at Virginia Beach in 1917. The lodge was dismantled in 1969, and its salvaged timber was used to build a Baptist building elsewhere in Virginia. *Courtesy of the author.*

Virginian-Pilot and *Portsmouth Star*. "I have been particularly interested because it explains some of the writing of Percy and the adventurers who landed near Cape Henry on April 26, 1607; it proves there was a wide inlet from the ocean into what is now Crystal Lake and on into Linkhorn Bay." This was the Gordon Hume property, a 130-acre tract that had stayed as naturally beautiful and pristine as the park next door. But she was worried, in retrospect, about the future of such an important tract in the face of the land grab that was going on beyond the already developed Oceanfront. What would happen, she must have wondered, if it were developed and the distinctive series of high ridges that went up from sea level about one hundred feet—running east and west and rising abruptly from low, marshy areas—was suddenly gone. The growth around them was already so dense that the height of the ridges, the undulation of their rise and fall into untouched marshes, was nearly imperceptible.

The area at the base of the Cape Henry lighthouses changed dramatically as America's involvement in World War II became inevitable. Fort Story, first established in 1914, underwent explosive development to accommodate a nation bracing for war. Construction of wartime quarters, office space and supply buildings such as those shown here (circa 1940) sprang up in the shadow of the lighthouses. *Virginian-Pilot* photographer Charles Borjes took this picture, and whether he used it for the newspaper or was taking photographs for the military is unknown. *Courtesy of the author.*

Men of the United States Navy Shore Patrol operated out of the Virginia Beach Police and Fire Station at 20th Street and Arctic Avenue during World War II; they posed in August 1944 for this photograph. Virginia Beach did not have a paid fire chief until Harry Russell Holland was hired in October 1928 along with two additional men. Police and fire were combined until 1947, three years after this picture was taken. On the reverse is a list of all men in the picture and their home of record, which does not universally imply birthplace. Kneeling (left to right) are Edward W. Jamison, Newark, New Jersey; H.C. Copeland, Atlanta, Georgia; Edward J. Bouchey, Hillman, Michigan; Nathan Freedman, New York City; Cecil C. McGraw, Beckley, West Virginia; George O. Harris, Baltimore, Maryland; N.C. Murdick, Indiana, Pennsylvania; Arthur L. Brightley, Washington, D.C.; Daniel P. Jett, Ivanhoe, Virginia; Joseph Indig, New York City; John H. Hoaster, Crown Point, Indiana; and J.J. Smith, Georgia. Standing (left to right) are W.A. Roberts, Wytheville, Virginia; Thomas Shirley Wheeler, Richmond, Virginia; James A. Ashbrook, Norwalk, Connecticut; Mark F. Connelly, Chicago, Illinois; Edward W. Gunia, Springdale, Pennsylvania; Donald R. Fortune, Philadelphia, Pennsylvania; J.G. Redmond, Baltimore, Maryland; John Stanley Courtney, Providence, Rhode Island; Ray C. Wilson, Catlett, Virginia; "Yours Truly," the original owner of the photo, from Rochester, New York, and also unidentified; Charles L. Williams, Bridgeton, New Jersey; Charles N. Tibbals, Thomaston, Connecticut; O.J. Gill, Memphis, Tennessee; Page L. Prillaman, Rocky Mount, Virginia; Felix Sobocinski, Salem, Massachusetts; William Hoffman, Minneapolis, Minnesota; Bernard G. Ballenger, Covington, Virginia; Paul W. Whittaker, Fries, Virginia; Charles W. Mullin, Philadelphia, Pennsylvania; James H. Brigham, Miami, Florida; A.B. Bowels, Bedford, Virginia; James F. Kelly, New York City; Anthony J. Lopez, Clarksburg, West Virginia; and William A. Baxter, Warrenton, North Carolina. The man sitting in the window is a Virginia Beach fireman. *Courtesy of the author.*

There was, centuries ago, a wide inlet between Cape Henry and The Cavalier Hotel, an opening clearly marked on Augustus Herman's 1673 map. Crystal Lake was part of this inlet. A creek connected it to Linkhorn Bay through Broad or Battses Bay before it continued on to the Lynnhaven River and from there to the Chesapeake Bay, making the land on which sit Seashore State Park, Fort Story and the Chesapeake Bay shore east of Lynnhaven inlet an island. Though it was closed by coastal storms long ago, it was a low-lying section between the old Avenue C and 66th Street that kept the ocean from entering Crystal Lake and remaking the inlet. The only breach reported of any significance in the twentieth century occurred during the 1933 hurricane. The sea rushed in and back out again. But had there been no homes and no streets there, the ocean might once again have opened up a hole in the shore to Crystal Lake, just two blocks inland.

The English who explored here in 1607 took safe harbor in Crystal Lake. The name closely associated with this lake should be familiar: Stratton's Creek. You will recall earlier mention of it in this narrative. An early settler named John Stratton was granted 150 acres of land between the east and south bay at Stratton's Creek in 1640. There was also an island in Broad Bay called Stratton's Island, renamed Lovett's Island. An early description of his property indicated that his tract was "nigh the head at the farthest side of the pine standing on the south side and running north, down the creek and easterly into the woods toward the sea." The 1695 map located in the Library of Congress offers confirmation that this would be the opening from Linkhorn Bay into Crystal Lake.

None of this ancient topography mattered much until developers carved out subdivisions and the county cut roads and built bridges to facilitate car traffic. Then it became the top topic of conversation. As developers started to disturb the shore to build, nearby residents started to notice the difference in the sand. Sand on the sea side, dug down far enough, brings up clay. This was not the case on Stratton's Creek. After digging here, only sand and more sand rose to the surface. This was the history of Stratton's Creek in the eighteenth and nineteenth centuries: it would regularly fill up with sand, and swampy marshland narrowed it until by the middle of the 1930s only a canoe or shallow-bottomed

The Bell House was built circa 1820 by Joshua James, who called it Cedar Grove; it is typical of antebellum houses but is the only one in old Princess Anne County that was built more like the plantation homes in the countryside of Maryland, particularly those around Hagerstown and Frederick. After James's death, his second wife, Maria, remarried to Alexander W. Bell, and it is from him that the home derives its current name. There were many owners after Bell, but in May 1942, Alfred T. Taylor and his family moved in. They renovated and added square footage to the house. The navy acquired the property in 1952, and the house, with few exceptions, has served as the official residence of the air station's commanding officer. *Official United States Navy Photograph.*

rowboat could navigate from Crystal Lake to Linkhorn Bay. But there was no one living there just then to complain. The only known house in the area was built about 1845 as a farmhouse.

Norfolk attorney and developer Hugh Davis bought his first parcel in what would become the Bay Colony subdivision in 1937. Bay Colony was built on the south side of the old creek on land that had once been owned by farmer William H. Rainey, son of John Shepherd and Nancy Padon Rainey. Three years after his father died in 1858, his mother married Thomas Keeling Cornick, and together he and Cornick continued to work the land. William Rainey died in 1914 at age seventy-three, long before he would have seen his farmland gobbled up for development. As

Bay Colony was developed on the south side of the old creek, the name Stratton's Creek was changed to Rainey's Gut, which entered Rainey's Pond, now Crystal Lake.

Land development on Crystal Lake's north shore led to the widening of the narrows between the lake and bay by the 1940s. Between the hills the English called mountains, deep canals were cut fifty to one hundred feet wide. A decade later, in the 1950s, there was little doubt left that the "swampy areas" dredged by developers for these deep canals were actually spring-fed creeks that flowed into the original inlet. This all occurred around the area now called Princess Anne Hills, where wildflowers blanketed the steep inclines to the water below, and giant pines, cut to complete construction, lay strewn along the builder's access road to his new canals.

Several dairy farms dotted Princess Anne County in the path of the navy's expansion of the Oceana air station, including the Rosemont Dairy, photographed on November 4, 1953. The navy kept the dairy operational to provide milk and dairy products for air station personnel and their families for a short period of time before the decision was reached to raze it. *Official United States Navy Photograph.*

"It was not hard to visualize," wrote Kyle, "Indians creeping through these woods to spy on the white men who had just landed from their strange large canoes for one felt far from civilization and the flat coastal beaches."

Princess Anne Hills gave up its name to the development carved from it. Charles Freeman Gillette—already nationally recognized as one of the premier landscape architects associated with the restoration and re-creation of historic gardens in the upper South and especially Virginia—spent a lengthy period of time walking the land and studying it before drawing a plat that he believed would not conflict with the natural beauty of the original Princess Anne Hills. Gillette could have drawn all day and still not conjured a plan that could protect this area. It had already been forested for project lumber and had unnatural canals dug through it in the place of spring-fed creeks; the landscape had already been touched and been permanently damaged. Further development in the 1950s that continued aggressively forward for more than two decades later leveled Princess Anne Hills. All of the trees were cut down in wide swaths, sparing only a few for new homes positioned strategically on the water, dividing the land into square lots.

More than a quarter century before all of this development at Bay Colony and Princess Anne Hills occurred, Kathleen Eveleth Bruce wrote a letter to the Norfolk newspapers in 1925 in which she begged that the Virginia Beach resort make use of names of historical significance in the designating of its place names. A few commercial property owners accepted her recommendation and named their establishments thusly, but mostly her suggestions fell on deaf ears. Fast-forward thirty years later, remarked Kyle, and the Princess Anne Hills development would blanket the subdivision with historic names. Roads running along the lakeshore and over the ridges were given names like Susan Constant, Godspeed and Discovery Ridge, for the three small ships that brought the English settlers to the Cape Henry shore in the spring of 1607. Sadly, after the "ridge" was worn down and no longer detectable, the word was dropped from the name of Discovery Road.

Virginia Beach reached a major crossroads when it came to the construction of roads and bridges. The development surge was accompanied by a population surge that overwhelmed existing roads and bridges in and out of the resort area in the 1950s and 1960s. Roads

At least one of Oceana's postwar commanding officers, Captain Joseph Quilter, had a soft spot for the nineteenth- and early twentieth-century farmhouses acquired by the navy and in the path of development as the base expanded after World War II. He observed that the farmhouse shown here was an elegant home and decided that it should be moved rather than be torn down. Quilter asked John Richey, base public works officer, how to move it, but before Richey could reply, Quilter came up with the idea of using log rollers. Trees were cut for rollers, the house was jacked off its foundation and the logs were placed underneath. The house was pulled down the road and on to the base's North Station next to Quilter's house. This picture was taken on April 13, 1951. Though Quilter thought that this particular house had charm, it and other farmhouses that he fought hard to move and adaptively reuse as officers' quarters were torn down as Oceana evolved into the master jet base it is today. *Official United States Navy Photograph.*

were woefully inadequate, and there were no bridges in locations that desperately needed them. But roads and bridges cost money that the resort did not have. After the opening of the Hampton Roads Bridge-Tunnel on November 1, 1957, Virginia Beach reaped the benefit of increased tourism but still needed better infrastructure to accommodate the rush of car traffic bound for the Oceanfront. There was no Virginia Beach–Norfolk Expressway to shoot them down to the shore, at least not yet. The old John A. Lesner Bridge that was first opened as a drawbridge across

Lynnhaven Inlet in 1928 was particularly antiquated, and it was raised so often to allow pleasure craft to pass that lengthy backups occurred on both sides of the bridge. A new bridge was built in its place in 1958. After the April 15, 1964 opening of the Chesapeake Bay Bridge-Tunnel, which connects Virginia Beach and Norfolk to Virginia's Eastern Shore, tourists had another route to the Oceanfront. When a second tube of the Hampton Roads Bridge-Tunnel was completed in 1976, Virginia Beach added a second span to the bridge to accommodate the commensurate increase in vehicular traffic coming off the bridge. Most of them never got much farther than the Virginia Beach resort during the season.

But out in the broad expanse of Princess Anne County, having survived the ebb and flow of fortune, it was still just then the repository of some of the nation's oldest homes and coveted landmarks before the tide of development swept many of them away. Concealed far down the county's rutted roads, deep in the folds of lush green woods and, sometimes, stashed away on a lonely finger of land along the Lynnhaven River were the brick-and-mortar relics of the county's first inhabitants and generations of those who followed. Even abandoned ruins standing in a foursquare of oaks were eerily beautiful. So were all of the family graveyards, with tombstones choked with weeds and stones standing silent watch.

Uncontrolled Growth

The January 26, 2011 *Virginian-Pilot* article title rang sadly familiar: "Huge Virginia Beach Church Gets OK on Development." Kempsville Presbyterian Church, which bought a 519-acre tract of the John Brown farm from real estate developers Steve and Art Sandler in 2009, had secured the Virginia Beach City Council's unanimous approval to build out the site according to the church's proposed plan at the council's January 25 meeting. Not everyone liked the project, including one member of the council, but after church leaders objected to planning guidelines for the tract, hired a lawyer and started to lobby council members to vote in their favor, the council acquiesced. The church got its way.

The victim this time was the last vestige of the old John Brown farm. The Brown tract is located near the city's municipal center in an area that Virginia Beach city planners have designated a transition area, a 4,700-acre swath of land that separates the city's rural south from its urban north. Aggressive development is not part of the plan for the transition area. In his redress of the council's church vote, Virginia Beach mayor William D. "Will" Sessoms, however, was clear. "This is a plan, and it's all about trying to come up with guidance for future development and plans do change."

Councilwoman Barbara Henley, who represents Virginia Beach's rural south, including the Brown tract, leveled her objection to the church's

This is 17th Street between Atlantic and Pacific, which has gained increasing importance at the resort since Virginia Beach Boulevard enjoined it in 1921 and the boulevard became the main route between Norfolk and the Oceanfront. The picture shown here was taken in the summer of 1946. The Morrison Building is the structure right foreground. *Courtesy of the author.*

plan for the open space. Kempsville Presbyterian's much-publicized development strategy is to hold back a seventy-acre parcel for church use and sell off the rest of the land for mixed-use development, including medical, office, institutional and retail use.

"Unfortunately," Henley opined in the January 16 *Virginian-Pilot* "the church plan calls for urbanized development." She observed that the church's project was the equivalent of plopping two Lynnhaven Malls into what has long been pastoral open space threaded with narrow country roads. Lynnhaven Mall is 1.17 million square feet. Two Lynnhaven Malls equates to 2.34 million square feet. Church officials envision 4 million square feet of development on the site. Picture the end result. One resident did. The *Pilot* quoted Dawn Flora, a North Landing Road resident, who rightly observed that Brown farm open space was "such a gem for the city." Flora went further to say, "You don't want to lose that. Everyone has their rights [the church], but as a whole you want to be cautious because once it's gone, it's gone."

City planners and City Manager James K. "Jim" Spore stood by the growth guidelines for the transition area. Planning staff had earlier informed the council that half of Kempsville Presbyterian's land should remain undeveloped as open space and that the total project should be capped at 2 million square feet. But the council's compromise on the Brown tract softened the language of the planning department's guideline for the transition zone and the property. Council's approval did not hold the church to the guideline to maintain open space on half of the land. The square footage restriction was still included but was watered down. Further development on the site might be permitted if road improvements are made. The church publicly stated that the development of the tract would bring immense financial return to the city of Virginia Beach.

Additional revenue in city coffers, though, does not buy a better quality of life for the people who live in the city. With every loss of open space, with every loss of a historic site, a little more of Virginia Beach's heritage and community character is lost. Money cannot buy them back. Lacking the political will to encroach the Green Line, the only area of compromise is the transition area. Certainly, the council's vote to allow the Kempsville Presbyterian's development plan to go forward opens the door to another developer to bargain the same terms on a future project. Once Pandora's box is opened, it is awfully hard to close.

The September 17, 2010 *Virginian-Pilot* reported that Virginia Beach identified eight parts of the city that council and staff have determined are due for a makeover; six of them fall along the old railroad corridor proposed for a light rail project. The objective in these strategic growth areas is intense urban-style development, going vertical with high-rise buildings to take advantage of limited developable land in the city's urban north. Lacking a redevelopment authority, the city is otherwise dependent on a landowner's willingness to sell his land to a private developer. This has been the Virginia Beach development model for decades. What happened to the old John Brown farm followed the model. Strategically situated between Naval Air Station Oceana and its outlying landing practice field, Naval Auxiliary Landing Field Fentress, seven miles southwest of Oceana in the city of Chesapeake, the Brown property that the Sandlers bought and banked for later development was once a large working farm.

Neptune's Seafood Restaurant ruled 31st Street and Atlantic Avenue, a corner that was aptly named Neptune's Corner for one of the Oceanfront's star eateries. This postcard, which provides two pictures of the restaurant, dates to circa 1950. *Courtesy of the author.*

Down the street from Neptune's Corner was Marty's Lobster House. Situated at the corner of 33rd Street and Atlantic Avenue, Marty's famous signage, similar to the familiar Coppertone advertisement of the period, is remembered even today though it has long since disappeared from the Virginia Beach landscape. Serving up some of the tastiest Maine lobster and Kansas City steaks at the Oceanfront, Marty's restaurant had strong numbers of locals and visitors following after World War II. This early postcard of Marty's dates to the late 1940s. *Courtesy of the author.*

Property and genealogical records indicate that the first John Brown in Princess Anne County was born in England in 1654 and died in the county, on his farm, in 1702. Subsequent generations of Browns continued to farm cotton and live off the land, which remained in the family through much of the twentieth century and for a brief time in the 1950s and 1960s was turned into a popular strawberry farm operated by Paul and Russell Brown. Between 1983 and 1984, most of the old Brown farm was sold for development. The City of Virginia Beach Public Schools built Centerville Elementary School on part of the Brown farm in 1984. The residential communities of Southgate, Hunt Club Forest and Chelsea Place were also developed on Brown land. Each development, school and church that pops up on any parcel of the old Brown farm has fallen within a tender buffer intended to safeguard the city's rural south, dotted with farmers' fields and horse farms, from the unchecked growth in the urban north.

Virginia Beach's so-called transition area is, in truth, an additional buffer to the city's better-known and no less controversial Green Line. When Virginia Beach City Council first drew its Green Line through the city in 1979, the objective was to stop unplanned, ugly sprawl that had, according to an August 21, 1996 *Virginian-Pilot* editorial, "spread like poison ivy through the northern part of the city, straining services and outpacing roads, sewers and water." The population explosion in the city's urban north cut a deep swath into early iterations of the Green Line, that crazy quilt of farms and open space that includes Princess Anne Courthouse, Lynnhaven, Pungo, Creeds, Blackwater, Sandbridge and Croatan, as well as lesser-known sections of southern Virginia Beach.

The city long ago ran out of clear land for new construction above the transition area and Green Line to satiate the demand of its bread-and-butter industries: real estate, defense and tourism. Virginia Beach is arguably the manifestation of textbook suburban sprawl. The city's housing boom in the 1970s, 1980s and 1990s produced miles of strip malls, big box stores and car dealerships that gobbled up massive acreage across its urban north. The footprints of nearly all of these massive commercial developments were accompanied by acres of unattractive parking lots. After taking in the scene, one reporter asked residents back in 1972 to picture Virginia Beach as a giant Monopoly board: "Then consider how it has grown or how the game began."

The game began with John Aragona, a land developer who bought property off Virginia Beach Boulevard near Chinese Corner in 1954—nine years before the Princess Anne County and city of Virginia Beach merger was consummated—and built single-family homes on it. For a man who earned as little as $1.50 a day when he came to the United States in 1923, it was payday to land on Aragona Village; he made $2 million and history, too. Aragona Village, completed in 1956, was the first planned subdivision between the city of Norfolk and the Atlantic Ocean. Certainly, as we know today, it was not the last. By the early 1970s, Virginia Beach was one of the fastest-growing cities in the commonwealth, with a population over 200,000 in March 1972. When compared to the United States Census figure of 172,000 for 1970, this meant a growth of 14,000 people per year.

Not everything was sunshine and calm seas for Virginia Beach at the beginning of the 1960s. The heated political fight between Norfolk and Princess Anne County over the merger that would marry the county to the resort town of Virginia Beach was getting ugly. Then Mother Nature dealt a blow far worse. The March 7, 1962 Ash Wednesday storm that struck the beach hard started two days before and moved across Virginia from the mountains at the far western tip of the state. Snow clouds traveled eastward, covering much of Virginia with wet, heavy snow. By the time it reached the coast, the storm had gained strength and struck a devastating blow to Virginia Beach. Waves between twenty and thirty feet and tides well over seven feet above mean high tide eroded the beach and destroyed significant sections of the boardwalk. Beachfront homes were among 340 houses in Virginia Beach that were severely damaged or completely destroyed by the Ash Wednesday storm. These homes, between 46th and 47th Streets, were pulled off their foundations and into the surf. *Courtesy of the author.*

Aragona foresaw the growth; he bought three additional farms in the county before the merger. County planners saw it, too, and predicted that Princess Anne's population would eventually exceed that of Suffolk. Three years after Aragona Village sprung from a farmer's field, planners' projections came true: a one-thousand-acre Bayside development added fifteen thousand people to the county census. Aragona Village was just the start. Planners began to change the housing mix and diversified the

The Virginia Beach Civic Center, better known as "the Dome," was built in 1958 on Pacific Avenue between 19th and 20th Streets, but in March 1963, city fathers renamed it the Alan B. Shepard Jr. Civic Center in honor of former Virginia Beach resident and astronaut Alan Shepard. The center, based on the design work of Buckminster Fuller, was the first aluminum geodesic dome constructed in the continental United States. Though it was considered nationally to be one of the city's most important buildings, the center was razed in September 1994 to make room for a municipal parking lot, which meant, in local parlance, a place for future development. This picture of the center was taken circa 1960 and bears a postal cancellation mark celebrating America's first space flight: Shepard's Mercury spacecraft *Freedom 7* suborbital flight, which took place on May 5, 1961. *Courtesy of the author.*

county's subdivision plan to include single-family, duplexes, apartments, townhouses, schools and religious facilities. Many of the city's planned unit developments built at the end of the 1970s and into the 1980s were self-sustaining, self-contained communities that provided commercial, recreation and religious facilities as part of the overall residential plan. Soon the city's residential growth outdistanced the economic rate of return. The city's uncontrolled growth soon became the number one topic during elections, boundary disputes and meetings to wrangle over infrastructure and city services that could no longer keep pace with development.

In other parts of the city, most especially the Great Neck section, the community's character and landscape underwent dramatic change starting in the middle of the 1970s. The 482-acre Broad Bay Manor development, situated near Frank W. Cox High School, was an upscale neighborhood, one of several that would soon pop up along both sides of Great Neck Road. Most of the homes in this area were sited on lots of one to one and a half to three acres or larger. Broad Bay Manor was carved out of the old John B. Dey farm, which also became the name of the elementary school built on his property. The development of these neighborhoods left less open space and pushed greater population density into parts of Virginia Beach that had heretofore been sparsely populated.

This kind of development was shocking to former Princess Anne County power brokers who had largely engineered and ensured the county's merger with the second-class city of Virginia Beach years before. "Who are all these people coming to Virginia Beach by the thousands each year?" asked a puzzled Sidney Kellam when interviewed for a June 23, 1977 *Ledger-Star* story. No one seemed to know the answer. The only certainty seemed to be their number: one thousand new neighbors every month. Suddenly, the close-knit Princess Anne family tree was becoming an amalgam of people from all over the United States and all over the world. Virginia Beach's Oceanfront was just the same. Locals were becoming scarce by the end of the 1970s.

After he retired from the navy in 1972, former Naval Air Station Oceana commanding officer Captain John Ellsworth Ford became a Virginia Beach real estate developer and construction company executive. As a young aviator, Ford first laid eyes on Oceana in 1955, three years after it had been designated an air station, and taken aboard its first jet aircraft. The air station's neighbors had just then begun to complain about jet noise and, once in a while, an occasional accident. Residential development was just starting to crop up on a country road here, a country road there. The air station was still isolated, surrounded by farm after farm, with a few homes built on either side of the railroad track near the old Oceana High School. After Ford took over as Oceana's commanding officer on September 4, 1970, everything had changed. Noise complaints had intensified, and so had the development around the air station.

"He was among the first strident voices calling for curtailment of development around the base," wrote the *Virginian-Pilot*'s Steve Stone after Ford's death in 1998. "Just as he had arrived, a major developer 'had built a little establishment of houses off the southwest end of Oceana.'" The subdivision was Magic Hollow, juxtaposed close to the end of Oceana's principal runway and built practically in the jet wash of the air station's complement of A-4 Skyhawks, A-6 Intruders and F-4 Phantoms that thundered by. Ford realized that most of the people complaining about jet noise had moved into the noise zone long after the air station rose from the mud flats of Princess Anne County nearly a decade and a half before it was designated an air station on April 1, 1952. He asked Virginia Beach City Council to curtail growth around Oceana. The members listened but did nothing. Unwilling to stop lucrative development deals from going through or get involved in owners' rights issues, the council turned a blind eye to Ford's request; what he was asking was not good business for the city.

Ford was later incredulous when the City of Virginia Beach permitted the development of Lynnhaven Mall. The mall was built, he opined, "in one of the most dangerous places they could [have built it] in the vicinity of the Oceana airfield." Aircraft bound for Oceana's runway make a downwind, 180-degree turn before landing just as they get on top of the mall. "In the whole pattern of launching and recovering aircraft, that is one of the danger points," he observed and Stone reported. "It doesn't mean that a crash is going to happen here; it just means that that's a place where it's more likely to happen."

The navy has exercised an abundance of caution in recent years regarding residential, recreational and commercial activities in its flight paths. One example is the recent decision to close Norfolk Naval Station's Fleet Recreation Park baseball fields, located off Hampton Boulevard and under the shadow of naval station's busy Chambers Field, to Little League play. A 2010 navy study concluded that the fields fell inside a clear zone, a "most likely" crash site to the runway, affirming the findings of a 1999 report. Despite the first finding more than a decade ago, the Fleet Park Little League was allowed to continue playing at the park. But on May 25, 2010, Captain Kelly M. Johnson, commanding officer of the Norfolk Naval Station, informed the Norfolk City Council that the 2011 Little League season would be the last at the park, saying that the potential for a crash in Fleet Park, located half a mile from the airstrip, is just too high to allow hundreds of children to play baseball and softball there.

The original Peppermint Beach Club, the iconic mainstay at 15th Street and Atlantic Avenue, was opened in the 1960s by Chester Louis Rodio, owner of many successful Virginia Beach businesses, including the Golden Garter, the Moonraker, Laskin Road Seafood and the Upper Deck Restaurant. But it was the Peppermint Beach Club, shown here on a period postcard, that gained fame as the "Home of Beach Music." The club regularly billed popular regional rock-and-roll headliners like Bill Deal and the Rhondels, Sebastian and the House Rockers and Little Willie and the Impressions, as well as national acts like Fats Domino, Roy Orbison and Joey D and the Starlighters. When the club was torn down on March 6, 1995, it was the last of the resort's shingle-style buildings, an architectural style that had once flourished at the Oceanfront from the 1880s and is now all but gone. *Courtesy of the author.*

When asked by Norfolk mayor Paul D. Fraim whether the definition of a crash zone had changed since 1994, it was reported in the *Virginian-Pilot* that Johnson replied, "I cannot speak for previous management. I don't know why they allowed entities like this [the Fleet Park Little League] to operate. They should not be allowed to operate in this area." A September 12, 2004 *Virginian-Pilot* report indicated that in Virginia Beach the navy had repeatedly notified the city of potential development problems in the Oceana crash zone. From 1975 to the middle of 2004, the Virginia Beach City Council ignored navy objections in nearly three out of every four votes, based on a review of navy letters and city records. But the navy also offered little or no resistance to housing developments in low- and medium-jet noise zones, and certainly within

The city of Virginia Beach had just been formed on January 1, 1963, from the merger of the town of Virginia Beach and the majority of old Princess Anne County when the November 1963 *Architectural Record* included an advertisement touting the flexibility and space-saving features of total electric design for Virginia Beach Public Schools. Key figures in the city's total electric school design were (left to right, foreground) Frank W. Cox, then superintendent of schools; J.C. Lindsey, superintendent of maintenance; and Ernest F. Stone, superintendent of construction. The men standing left to right in the background include B.S. Martin, Virginia Electric and Power Company representative; John S. Waller, of Waller and Britt, Architects; and Denard L. Gusler, Professional Engineer, of Vansant and Gusler, Consulting Engineers. They are standing in front of Plaza Elementary School, built in 1961. Cox became superintendent of Princess Anne County public schools in 1933 and kept the position when the town and county merged; he retired in 1968. *Courtesy of the author.*

the clear zone, around Oceana until 2003. Go back to what Ford stated with regard to Lynnhaven Mall. Then go back to the description of Kempsville Presbyterian's mixed-use development plan for the old Brown farm. The church's land is right in the middle of the flight path between Oceana and Fentress, but because there was no residential use planned, Oceana's spokeswoman Kelley Stirling called it "compatible" with the navy's interest.

In truth, the navy and the City of Virginia Beach offered no resistance to commercial and residential development under Oceana's flight path until it was learned on December 22, 2003, that land encroachment issues, such as those plaguing Oceana, should be considered in the next round of base closures. The Oceana air station subsequently became the target of the 2005 federal Base Realignment and Closure (BRAC) Commission. After reading BRAC decisions to close several key naval air stations, some members of the Virginia Beach community strongly lobbied to have the navy's F/A-18 Hornet reassigned to Oceana from Naval Air Station Jacksonville, Florida, and in so doing vowed to curb commercial and residential encroachment under Oceana's flight path. The BRAC Commission added Oceana to the military's list of endangered bases on July 19, 2005. The seven-to-one vote stunned state and local officials, many of whom had predicted that the commission would not put Oceana into the mix of bases being considered for closure; it is, after all, the navy's East Coast master jet base and Virginia Beach's largest employer.

The commission order that came down to the city in December 2005 provided detailed directions to implement new rules intended to halt development in certain areas around Oceana, known as Accident Potential Zone 1 (or APZ-1), a 1,600-acre area that the navy determined was incompatible with flight operations. The one issue that remained a challenge to the city was the order to roll back encroachment by incompatible uses in APZ-1 and the clear zone. The BRAC order states that the city is to "purchase and condemn" incompatible use property in the APZ-1 areas around Oceana for the purpose of preventing further encroachment. In its best effort to satisfy this requirement without going through the protracted process of condemning 3,400 homes, the city adopted new zoning laws on December 20 to preclude future incompatible development.

Despite the city's quick move to satisfy BRAC instruction, in early 2006 the Pentagon warned the state and the City of Virginia Beach that their efforts to limit commercial and residential development near Oceana Naval Air Station "may not fully address" the demands of the BRAC Commission. The likely reason for this warning is clear. While the city plan, on paper, calls for controlling and rolling back incompatible development of the land beneath the flight path between Oceana and Fentress, which it calls the Oceana Land Use Conformity Program, it also speeds up the process for commercial development—of which, again, the Brown farm tract is the most recent example. The city's "added commitment" to make the Oceana program work includes provisions for faster development approvals; waivers of development fees and utility hookup fees; tax incentives; economic development incentives; and facilitating the purchase, exchange and lease of property. How long Oceana can remain viable in Virginia Beach is largely dependent on the city honoring its commitment to roll back existing encroachment and mitigate further commercial and residential development under the air station's flight path. Certainly, recent history would indicate that commercial development has continued in the corridor of concern and with unanimous approval of the city council.

Down at the Virginia Beach resort, keeping tourists coming back between Memorial Day and Labor Day has come at an equally high price. There is little hint of the small-town charm displayed in pictures of old cottages, hotels and inns that once stood lockstep on the beach at the turn of the twentieth century. New hotels, restaurants and entertainment venues took their place. Often little consideration was afforded the historic and cultural value of the old places that have come down from the end of World War II and continue to be threatened today. Conservation and adaptive reuse of treasured pieces of the fabric of old Virginia Beach did not, in large measure, ever come to fruition. The large number of significant structures and landscapes in the county and down at the Virginia Beach Oceanfront before World War II versus the comparably small number of historic houses and resort buildings granted a reprieve from the wrecking ball since the last half of the twentieth century is evidence enough that preservation was not the priority.

When the iconic Peppermint Beach Club was razed on March 6, 1995, two important pieces of Virginia Beach history went with it: the building itself and the club that was its last tenant. The 1907 shake-clad building at 15th Street and Atlantic Avenue was among a handful of surviving examples of Virginia Beach's shingle-style buildings, popular from the 1880s; in 1924, it became the home of the New Ocean Casino, which gave its address as between 14th and 16th Streets. The Peppermint Beach Club was opened by Pennsylvania native Chester Louis Rodio.

Rodio was one of those returning World War II airmen who came home with the dream of starting his own business. He moved to Virginia Beach in 1949, when Atlantic Avenue was still just a few hotels, restaurants and boardinghouses. Here, he opened his first restaurant, the Doll House, on the corner of 14th Street and Atlantic Avenue, where he sold the best hot dogs and chili at the beach. He eventually engaged in many other successful restaurants and clubs, including the Golden Garter, the Moonraker, Laskin Road Seafood and the Upper Deck Restaurant. But the business for which he is best known is the original Peppermint Beach

Built just after World War II, the Jefferson Hotel was located at the corner of 19th Street and Atlantic Avenue and is shown on this circa 1960 advertising postcard. Though the Jefferson is gone in name, the building still stands and has been repurposed as a hotel and beach mall. *Courtesy of the author.*

Club, known as the "Home of Beach Music" and the place that started the public dance hall craze at Virginia Beach in the 1960s. The club regularly billed popular regional rock-and-roll headliners like Bill Deal and the Rhondels, Sebastian and the House Rockers and Little Willie and the Impressions.

Just before the Peppermint was taken down, an auction of the club's contents was held on February 9, 1995; it was there that Vick Sands, who had once booked musical talent for Oceanfront clubs, told *Virginian-Pilot* reporter Tom Holden what the Peppermint embodied. "It's the memories; that's it, the memories. If you could somehow write about the people who met here, who fell in love and who are now grandparents themselves, man, that would be a great story. It's all about the memories." John Vakos, who had once managed the long-gone Top Hat at 29th Street and Atlantic Avenue, was there, too. When he saw Sands, he offered this: "There's a lot of history here. There are businessmen from all over Tidewater who once played here." While the Top Hat was replaced by the Ocean Front Inn, the Peppermint was torn down for a parking lot.

These young women posed playfully in the surf at Virginia Beach in 1960. *Courtesy of the author.*

In the two years before the Peppermint's last call, the Oceanfront lost the Avamere, a charming 1950s-era hotel famous for its front porch rocking chairs, laidback southern hospitality and its neighbor the Halifax Hotel and, farther down the strip, the 1944 Sea Escape Motel. But the most significant loss of all was the Virginia Beach Civic Center, better known as "the Dome." Built in 1958 on Pacific Avenue between 19th and 20th Streets, the city's first civic center was based on the design work of Buckminster Fuller and was the first aluminum geodesic dome constructed in the continental United States. In 1963, it was named the Alan B. Shepard Jr. Civic Center in honor of the *Mercury 7* astronaut and former Virginia Beach resident.

The Dome opened at the dawn of rock-and-roll, and as we were reminded in Roberta Thisdell's June 30, 1993 *Virginian-Pilot* retrospective, it played an important role as "midwife to the British Invasion, psychedelic,

Motown, surf, heavy metal and just a little punk." For a place that could only seat one thousand, concerts by legendary performers Chuck Berry, Johnny Mathis, Ray Charles, the Beach Boys, Diana Ross and the Supremes, Jimi Hendrix, The Who and the Rolling Stones were close-up affairs. Hendrix, The Who and the Rolling Stones blew the doors off the place. Before it was torn down in September 1994, the Dome was considered nationally as one of Virginia Beach's most important buildings, a status that could not save it from the wrecking ball. A parking lot also took its place.

There is an old saying that a man is largely what his memories are. Memories are about all we have left of the Virginia Beach that many of us knew and loved. The Virginia Beach of yesteryear is all but gone, and the fabric of that old Princess Anne County crazy quilt has been broken many times over by the pace of uncontrolled growth that continues to spread like poison ivy over the city. We might understand better what happened to our beloved Virginia Beach if we could go back and have a chat with city native and raconteur Cornelia Randall Holland, daughter of the resort town's first mayor, Bernard Peabody Holland. Fortunate for

Shake-clad cottages and the Oceanfront's old casinos and bathhouses had given way mid-century to modern hotels, motels and eateries when this picture of the beach in front of the Princess Anne Inn, located at 25th Street and Atlantic Avenue, was made into a postcard, mailed on July 10, 1971. *Courtesy of the author.*

all of us, Bill Morris did just that for a June 13, 1980 *Virginian-Pilot* article he wrote about her. In it she offered this insight: "People ask me why I stay. Well, they've torn down everything. If I sold this house they'd have it torn down by eight o'clock the next morning. I stay because it's home." Cornelia was almost ninety when she died on February 12, 1988. She was right about her house: it was razed after her death.

The last old cottage on the Oceanfront is the home that Cornelia's father built for her mother, the former Emily Randall Gregory, in 1895; he called it the Brick House. Cornelia's mother did not care for the sound of waves breaking on the shore, so Bernard Holland built a larger house for his wife across the street, one block inland, that he called Ozone. The first Virginia Beach mayor's office was located in the library of this house. He sold the cottage to Norfolk businessman Cornelius deWitt in 1909, and it has been known as the deWitt Cottage ever since. The deWitts called it Wittenzand, Dutch for "white sand." DeWitt enlarged the cottage to twenty-two rooms in 1917; it remained in the family until 1988. With its fourteen-inch-thick walls, twenty-two rooms, basement and attic, the cottage is a good example of an early beach house. Listed on the Virginia Landmarks Register, it is presently the home of the Atlantic Wildfowl Heritage Museum and the Back Bay Wildfowl Guild. The deWitt Cottage is the last remaining late nineteenth-century beach house at Virginia Beach. The 1903 lifesaving station is still there, too. Today, it is the home of the old Coast Guard Station Museum at 24th Street and the Boardwalk. The rest of Virginia's front porch by the sea is gone. All of it is just a memory now.

Author's Note

A s you look back through the photographs in this book, take note of the photographer who took each picture. Beyond the narrative, they give renewed meaning to the phrase "a picture is worth a thousand words." There are five primary photographers whose work was included in the final edit of the book, and what follows is intended to provide you with more information about each one, as well as why their work and not others fills these pages. Their work is critically important to telling the visual backstory of Virginia Beach, and while all of them are long since gone, the work endures and continues to inform. To make the introduction, they are, lady first: Frances Benjamin Johnston, Charles Simpson Borjes, Charles Clyde Ebbets, Henry William Gillen and Harry Cowles Mann. Ebbets's photograph "Dianas of the Beach" is on the cover.

Frances Benjamin Johnston, who went by the nickname Fannie, was born on January 15, 1864, in Grafton, West Virginia, to wealthy and well-connected parents, Anderson Doniphan and Frances Antoinette Benjamin Johnston. The family moved to Washington, D.C., in 1872, where her father took a position in the United States Department of Treasury. Fannie went abroad many times during her life, one of the first to study art at Académie Julian in Paris, France, between 1883 and 1885. Shortly after she returned home, she helped form the Art Students League of Washington, D.C., which later was incorporated as the

Corcoran Gallery School. Though she had a passion for art, particularly illustration, she was drawn to photography as a more accurate medium to convey what she saw. Close family friend George Eastman, inventor of the handheld camera and other photographic devices, gave Fannie her first camera. She learned photography and darkroom techniques from the best when Thomas Smillie, director of photography for the Smithsonian Institution, took her under his wing. She opened her own photographic studio in Washington, D.C., in 1895, taking portraits of her famous contemporaries, among them Susan B. Anthony, Mark Twain and Booker T. Washington. Fannie traveled in the same elite society to which she was born, and when she got the magazine assignment to take celebrity portraits, like those of Anthony, Twain and Washington, she was quickly crowned the "photographer to the American court."

Gender never held Fannie back. She was fiercely independent and unconventional. Her mother, Frances Johnston, had been a Congressional journalist for the *Baltimore Sun*, and her daughter built quickly on her familiarity with the Washington political scene to secure the best assignments, among them the George Grantham Bain News Service. Bain, who was also her agent, gave her an early "scoop" to take photographs of Admiral George Dewey, the "Hero of Manila Bay," on the deck of his flagship, USS *Olympia*, while it was at anchor in the harbor of Naples, Italy, in 1899. When the navy balked at a female photographer coming aboard an American warship, Fannie, as the story has been told, located her friend, then assistant secretary of the navy Theodore Roosevelt, at his home in Oyster Bay, New York, and got a letter of introduction that was forwarded to Admiral Dewey. She got the picture.

Fannie knew how to "work the room" of the nation's capital with deft that has arguably never been repeated. She was the official White House photographer for the Benjamin Harrison, Grover Cleveland, William McKinley, Theodore Roosevelt and William Howard Taft administrations. She photographed events such as world's fairs and peace treaty signings and took the last portrait of President William McKinley at the Pan American Exposition of 1901 just before his assassination. During her successive White House assignments, Fannie's photographs were exhibited in the finest museums in the United States and Europe, including czarist Russia. She received the gold medal and grand prix at the Paris Universal Exposition in 1900 and the Palmes Académiques from the French government in 1905. Her Paris Universal Exposition prize was awarded for her photographs of the buildings and students of the Hampton Normal and Agricultural Institute in Hampton, Virginia, a commission she had received from Hollis Burke Frissell, the second principal of Hampton Institute, in 1899. This series, displayed as "Exposé nègre" at the exposition, is considered by her biographers as some of Fannie's most telling work. By 1913, already a widely acclaimed photographer, she opened a gallery in New York City.

In the 1920s, Fannie became increasingly interested in photographing architecture, moved by the desire to document historic buildings and gardens falling into disrepair and about to be redeveloped or lost. Her photographs remain an important resource for modern architects, historians and preservationists. She exhibited a series of 247 photographs of Fredericksburg, Virginia, that showed the decay and disrepair of historic mansions of the wealthy and the ramshackle shacks of a sharecropper. This 1928 exhibit was titled Pictorial Survey—Old Fredericksburg, Virginia—Old Falmouth and Nearby Places and was described as "a series of photographic studies of the architecture of the region dating by tradition from Colonial times to circa 1830" as a "historical record and to preserve something of the atmosphere of an old Virginia town."

Publicity from this display prompted the University of Virginia to hire Fannie to document its buildings and the State of North Carolina to employ her to record its architectural history. Subsequent to these assignments, the State of Louisiana hired her to document its huge inventory of rapidly deteriorating plantation properties. She received successive grants from the Carnegie Corporation of New York to document southern architecture in the 1930s, including sites in Virginia and seven other states, all of which were given to the Library of Congress for public use. As noted in the Library of Congress's overview of the Carnegie Survey of the Architecture of the South Collection, Johnston "was one of the first to document vernacular building traditions, photographing not only the great mansions of the South, but churches, graveyards, row houses, offices, kitchens, warehouses, mills, shops, farm buildings, and inns." For her incredible work in preserving old and endangered buildings, Fannie was named an honorary member of the American Institute of Architects.

Fannie Johnston penned a widely read article for *Ladies Home Journal* in 1897 in which she observed that photography as a profession should appeal "particularly to women" and that in it there are great opportunities "for a good-paying business—but only under very well defined conditions. The prime requisites—as summed up in my mind after long experience and thought—are these," she wrote. "The woman who makes photography profitable must have, as to personal qualities, good common sense, unlimited patience to carry her though endless failures, equally unlimited tact, good taste, a quick eye, a talent for detail, and a genius for hard work." She was brilliant with the detail. Her work, largely included here in chapter two, is part of a much larger collection of photographs of old Princess Anne County properties now held in the Library of Congress. From these pictures you can see firsthand the detail for which she was, and is, famous. Fannie Johnston was at the top of her profession for decades—part of a renowned and talented handful of the nation's first female photographers and photojournalists—when she died in New Orleans, Louisiana, on May 16, 1952, at the age of eighty-eight.

Harry Cowles Mann was born on June 8, 1866, in Petersburg, Virginia, to Judge Edwin Murray and Patty Cowles Mann. Mann did not become a professional photographer until he was forty years old. We know that his younger brother, Colonel James Mann, was counsel to the Jamestown Photographic Corporation, the organization responsible for taking the official photographs of the 1907 Jamestown Tercentennial Exposition, when Harry was hired as an apprentice photographer on a staff of seasoned cameramen from whom he would learn his trade. His apprenticeship did not last long. Harry Mann's exposition pictures are easy enough to distinguish from those whose talents did not quite measure up to his own.

Far less is known about Harry Mann's personal life than his commercial photography career. The first camera he used to take pictures of Cape Henry's virgin pine stands, the Desert and nearby bays and creeks was a simple four-by-five plate camera. After good success marketing and selling his prints, he soon bought two eight-by-ten and two five-by-seven plate cameras, and it was from these larger-format cameras that he took the most extraordinary pictures of Cape Henry and the area surrounding it. *National Geographic* published Mann's work between 1915 and 1918, including his Cape Henry photographs, many of which are included here, in the magazine's September 1915 issue. These pictures are indicative of Mann's ability to take his craft to the level of art form. Mann's Cape Henry photogravures won him accolades and prizes from Paris to London to New York. Most of Mann's photographs are located in chapters one and three.

From his large body of work, it is easy enough to draw the conclusion that Harry Mann shared not only Fannie Johnston's reputation for detail and clarity but also her passion for documenting historic structures and landscapes. Between 1907 and 1923, Mann was one of Virginia's most prolific and important photographers. From the moment he took his first picture, this quiet and often frail man was destined to change the way we see the world. He died on December 12, 1926, at the State Colony for Epileptics and Feeble-minded in Lynchburg, Virginia.

Henry William Gillen was born in New York City on August 22, 1887, to William and Martha Newman Gillen. Gilly ran away from home at the age of thirteen and quickly lost touch with his family. No one is certain what his life was like before he made a name for himself as a pioneer motion picture camera operator and nationally known commercial photographer sometime after 1900. He worked for the largest pictorial news syndicates in New York and Chicago before coming to Norfolk sometime in 1912, first as a Pathe Company cameraman.

During his first years in Norfolk, Gilly was associated with Paramount and Artcraft and other studios around the city. During World War I, he was a photographer in the United States Army. He returned to the city in 1918 and opened his own studio, Acme Photo Company, and from this enterprise his reputation as one of the nation's best chroniclers with a camera was solidified. Gilly is in this writer's family tree. After he returned from his stint as an army photographer, he married Annie Lee Satchell, the first cousin once removed of my great-uncle, Carroll Weldon Cavender, who was married to my grandfather's sister, Mary Lanetta Fentress. Gilly died in Norfolk on November 14, 1951. His photos of the Croatan Club, Courtney Terrace and the Cavalier Country Club are spread throughout chapters two and three.

Charles Clyde Ebbets was born on August 18, 1905, in Gadsden, Alabama, the son of Samuel Clyde and Ailene West Ebbets. Unlike Harry Mann, Ebbets got his first camera at the age of eight when he charged it to his mother's drugstore account. Like Gillen, he became involved in early motion picture work, both in front of and behind the camera. For a brief time, perhaps less than a year, in 1924, he acted in low-budget motion pictures. For the balance of the 1920s, he was employed at various times as a pilot, wing walker, race car driver, wrestler and hunter. There was nothing he could not do and nothing that he would not try. Ebbets gained early notoriety as the official photographer for prizefighter Jack Dempsey and also as staff photographer for the *Miami Daily News.*

Ebbets took his most iconic photograph ("Lunchtime Atop a Skyscraper") after he was hired to take pictures of New York City's Rockefeller Center under construction in 1932. But by then he had already gained an international reputation as one of the nation's top photographers, propelled to fame by having his photographs published in every major newspaper and magazine in the United States, including the prestigious *New York Times* and *National Geographic.* From the summer of 1932, and for several years to come, he covered sports and the social scene in Miami, Augusta, Virginia Beach and New York City. Chambers of commerce and local advertising boards paid him to take pictures later used to promote tourism. This was big business, even during the Great Depression.

After 1933, with the exception of contract work that took him out of state, Ebbets lived and worked in Florida for the rest of his life, his interests drawn to the growth of Orange State tourism, Seminole Indian culture and the untouched, extraordinarily beautiful Everglades. Two years after he moved permanently to Florida, in 1935, Ebbets became the first official Associated Press photographer in the state. That same year, his photos of the 1935 Labor Day hurricane that devastated the Florida Keys were circulated worldwide. During this same period, we know that he also founded the Miami Press Photographers Association and was its first president.

After he broke his back on a photo shoot in the Everglades, Ebbets was ineligible to serve in the military during World War II. But because he was a licensed pilot and a photographer, he served as an attaché to the Army

Air Corps Special Services and would later be assigned to Embry-Riddle Aeronautical Institute, which at that time was training pilots of both the American and British Royal Air Forces. During the war, he documented all phases of base development and personnel training in Florida and spent time in South America working under General Henry Harley "Hap" Arnold, who oversaw the training of American and British pilots at bases in Brazil. Ebbets went home to Miami after the war and became one of the three founders of the City of Miami Publicity Bureau. For the next seventeen years, he was the chief photographer for the City of Miami. He died in Miami on July 14, 1978. Ebbets's pictures of Virginia Beach are featured in chapter four.

Charles Simpson Borjes was born in Norfolk on November 25, 1891, the son of Charles and Gertrude Russell Borjes. Charlie Borjes's father was a musician and, later, symphony director born in New York to German immigrant parents who were also musicians, as were all of his father's brothers. The Borjeses eventually filled their Brambleton home with six boys and one girl; Charlie was the oldest. Those who knew him informed this writer many years ago that Charlie's sense of humor and dry wit were the products of growing up in a house where practical jokes and laughter were the norm, not the exception. In his late teens, becoming a press photographer hadn't crossed his mind. He was a gifted athlete who wanted to play professional baseball. After a devastating injury to his ankle, Charlie traded a baseball bat for a camera. With the exception of his two-year service with the Norfolk Light Artillery Blues on the Mexican border during World War I, Charlie worked for the *Virginian-Pilot* newspaper as a photographer from 1913 to 1956.

Charlie's talent with a camera left little doubt that he was the most gifted photographer on the newspaper staff from the day he started. As new photographers came through the newsroom, he showed them his Graflex Speed Graphic camera, crammed into an old canvas bag, informing them that their chances of success improved if they "could only abandon all these modern gadgets and get back to grassroots photographic principles." That was Charlie. His pictures are distinguished by what Norfolk raconteur George Holbert Tucker long ago called Charlie's "unerringly sensitive photographic sense" and attention to detail and clarity. He was, without question, the finest sports photographer in

Virginia during his active career with the Norfolk newspapers. He took photos for the newspaper for so long that his pictures are sprinkled into chapters one and four and represent the breadth of subject matter for which he was best known.

Former *Virginian-Pilot* reporter and, later, entertainment editor Warner Twyford use to enjoy telling good Charlie Borjes stories; they worked together often, and Twyford got to see him in action. It was always a show. "Charlie's camera," he once said, "has led him into more adventures than Alice's white rabbit did for her." Such was the circumstance when Charlie's editor sent him down to Norfolk's Elmwood Cemetery to take a picture of the huge white marble John Harvey and Martha Core Mausoleum, the largest and most expensive mausoleum in any of the city's cemeteries. The picture would run on the Sunday morning second front. For one reason or another, he didn't get around to getting the picture until late Saturday afternoon. By the time he arrived on his bicycle, the cemetery gate was locked for the night. The only way he was going to get a nighttime shot was to set off a pan of flash powder. Keep this in mind as you read on.

After Charlie sized up the task of getting the picture, he figured that the nighttime photo would be more dramatic. He vaulted over the hedge to get the shot. Then he started to take notice of the neighbors, the living ones whose homes backed up to the cemetery east of the mausoleum. He could hear music, people laughing, children playing and suppers cooking. Charlie smiled in appreciation because he always liked to see folks have a good time. Without giving it a second thought, he set up his camera and loaded his flash gun with an extra charge of powder to make it flood the final photograph with dark and light contrast. He stepped back, not anticipating the effect an overcharged flash might have on the neighborhood.

"He pulled the trigger," George Tucker later wrote, "the blinding flash, a miniature Hiroshima, got the picture Charlie wanted all right, but it also produced results he wasn't counting on." There was audible silence, soon replaced by noise of frightened people fleeing from their homes. Charlie knew little about it; he had scurried off to the newspaper to print his picture. Wondering what all the night's hoopla was about, he got curious and pedaled back to the neighborhood to find it deserted.

Every writer has a favorite story about a person he has brought to life, and while it is hard to choose one about Charlie, his misadventure with the Norfolk Fire Department makes a good yarn to end this chapter. Charlie was sent down to cover a ship fire at the Water Street dock. He climbed onto the roof of a nearby warehouse to get a better shot of the action from above. Just as he always did, he set up his camera and started to fill his flash pan with a powder charge, which soon set off a boom that sounded like Fourth of July fireworks to him. But he did not know that it sounded far worse from below. A collective cry went up: "My God. It's spread to the warehouse!" The next he knew, Charlie was looking over the edge of the roof staring down at upturned fire hoses. He broke into a run toward the far end of the warehouse to beat the water spray coming in his direction. But he didn't make it. He hit a soft spot in the warehouse roof and plunged through. Charlie would have gone straight down, but he spread his elbows and hung on. "Scared me to death and skinned my knees," he said later. "But the stream of water passed over just then and missed me." This "grandmaster of Virginia press photographers" spent forty-one years telling the story of all of us one picture at a time. He died on May 23, 1959, in Portsmouth, Virginia, less than three years after his retirement.

Select Bibliography

Primary Sources, Articles, Pamphlets, Papers, Reports and Speeches

There were numerous primary sources and articles, brochures, pamphlets, meeting minutes, wills, deeds, court proceedings, correspondence, early Virginia religious petitions, letters and papers in the Library of Congress, organization papers and broadsides that informed the author; most were dated but some were not. A select few of these informative references are listed below, while others have been included, where practical, in the text.

Alley, Jerry. "Virginia Beach: 1,000 New Neighbors Each Month." *Ledger-Star*, June 23, 1977.

Applegate, Aaron. "Beach, Council Split by Church's Land Plans." *Virginian-Pilot*, January 16, 2011.

———. "Huge Virginia Beach Church Gets OK on Development." *Virginian-Pilot*, January 26, 2011.

———. "Virginia Beach's Plan to Transform the City." *Virginian-Pilot*, September 7, 2010.

Archer, Gabriel. *A Relatyon of the Discovery of Our River, from James Fort into the Maine, Made by Captain Christopher Newport, and Sincerely Written by a Gent, of the Colony* (covering the period May 21 to June 22, 1607) in Barbour, Philip L., ed. *The Jamestown Voyages Under the First Charter 1606–1609.* 2nd series. Cambridge, UK: Cambridge University Press, 1969.

Bancroft, Raymond L. "Norfolk Requests to Join Merger: Kellam Hedges Opinion." *Virginian-Pilot,* November 9, 1961.

———. "Princess Anne Nudged on Water." *Virginian-Pilot,* May 30, 1962.

Barrow, Mary Reid. "An Historic Revival after Years of Neglect, the Ferry Plantation House Will Be Renovated, Preserving 300 Years of Local History." *Virginia Beach Beacon,* July 26, 1996.

———. "Venerable Cottage Being Spared for a New Life as a Restaurant." *Virginia Beach Beacon,* April 23, 1995.

Blackford, Frank. "Born in the '20s, but Reaching for the '70s." *Virginian-Pilot,* June 27, 1971.

Borjes, Russell. "It Was the Start of Something Big." *Virginian-Pilot,* April 16, 1972.

Bouvier, Leon, and Sharon McCloe Stein. "Virginia's Population in 2050: Paying the Price for Uncontrolled Growth." Negative Population Growth. http://www.npg.org/polls091200/va_paper.html.

Bruce, Kathleen Eveleth. "Down on Lynnhaven." *Norfolk Ledger-Dispatch,* April 14, 16–19, 25–26, 28 and 30, 1924, and May 2–3, 1924.

———. "Virginia Beach: Chance to Emphasize Our Historical Priority over Every Other English-speaking Settlement." *Virginia Beach Ledger,* October 6, 1925.

City of Virginia Beach. "Historic Resources Management Plan 1994." http://www.vbgov.com/file_source/dept/planning/Document/HistoricResourcesManagmentPlan.pdf.

Crist, Helen. "Old Fairfield House to Be Demolished." *Virginia Beach Sun*, February 17, 1972.

Dorsey, Jack, and Dale Eisman. "Oceana Comes Out a Winner." *Virginian-Pilot*, March 1, 1995.

Friends of Ferry Plantation House. http://www.ferryplantation.org.

Giametta, Charles. "Virginia Beach Celebrates 20th Anniversary." *Virginian-Pilot*, January 2, 1983.

Guagenti, Tom. "A Noisy Neighbor—New Hornet Squadrons Have Divided Beach Residents into Two Camps: One Side Salutes Their Mission while the Other Protests Their Presence." *Virginian-Pilot*, November 28, 1999.

Hartig, Dennis. "Past Mistakes Haunt Ferry Farm Proposal." *Virginia Beach Beacon*, April 15–16, 1987.

Holden, Tom. "The Oceanfront's Next Casualty; Club May Be Demolished; the Peppermint, in Bad Repair at Age 88, Would Join Historic Buildings Meeting the Wrecking Ball." *Virginian-Pilot*, September 29, 1994.

———. "Oceanfront Auction Raises Money, Fond Memories; Old Friends Gather to Swap Tales and Pick up Bargains at the Peppermint Beach Club." *Virginian-Pilot*, February 10, 1995.

Holland, Ann Francis. "The Odd Couple." No date. http://freepages.genealogy.rootsweb.ancestry.com/~knower/oddcouple.htm.

Jaffe, Margaret Davis. "Princess Anne County Rich in Colonial Remains." *Virginian-Pilot and Norfolk Landmark*, February 28, 1926.

Kyle, Louisa Venable. "A Countrywoman's Scrapbook: Cavalier William Moseley." *Virginian-Pilot*, January 19, 1958.

————. "Descendants of William Moseley Provided Princess Anne County with Proud Heritage." *Virginian-Pilot* and *Portsmouth Star*, January 22, 1956.

————. "The Strangest Honeymoon at Virginia Beach Took Place Aboard a Shipwrecked Schooner." *Virginian-Pilot*, April 15, 1956.

La Gorce, John Oliver. "The Warfare on Our Eastern Coast." *National Geographic* 28, no. 3 (September 1915).

Ledger-Star. "Preservation Plan Urged for Beach." September 19, 1987.

Lipper, Bob. "Proud Era Vestiges Remain." *Virginian-Pilot*, December 15, 1974.

McAllister, Bill. "Martin Urges Talks to Merge Norfolk and Virginia Beach." *Virginian-Pilot*, June 14, 1967.

Minium, Harry, and Lia Russell. "Navy to Norfolk Little Leaguers: Find a New Home." *Virginian-Pilot*, May 27, 2010.

Morris, Bill. "Past Laps around Beach Survivor." *Virginian-Pilot*, June 13, 1980.

Murphy, John. "Oceana Growth Would Be Payoff of 4-year Crusade." *Virginian-Pilot*, September 14, 1997.

Naval Air Station Oceana, Virginia Beach & BRAC. "The Solution." http://www.bracresponse.com/solution.html.

New York Times. "Princess Anne Hotel Burns." June 10, 1907.

New York Tribune. June 11, 1863.

Norfolk Ledger-Dispatch. "Cornerstone of New Cavalier Hotel Is Laid." Virginia Beach edition, May 9, 1926.

Norfolk Virginian. "Watering Place that Is to Be." August 14, 1881.

Official Publication of the Norfolk Chamber of Commerce 19, no. 11 (November 1957).

Oxford Dendrochronology Laboratory. "The Tree-Ring Dating of the Adam Keeling House, Virginia Beach, Virginia." Interim report, December 2006.

Parker, Stacy. "This Old House: Beach Cottage Once Occupied by Life Saver." *Virginian-Pilot,* November 10, 2009.

Reed, Bill. "Razing Comes to the Peppermint: A Venerable Beach Club Joins the Dome and Two Old Hotels in the Pages of History." *Virginia Beach Beacon,* March 10, 1995.

Sewell, Kay Doughtie. "Her Oldest Resident Recalls 71 years at Virginia Beach." *Virginian-Pilot,* March 25, 1956.

Smith, John. *Map of Virginia with a Description of the Country, the Commodities, People, Government and Religion.* London, 1612. http://www.virtualjamestown.org/johnsmithsmap.html.

Stone, Steve. "Chester Rodio, an Original Virginia Beach Boy, Dies at 86." *Virginian-Pilot,* May 18, 2008.

———. "Former Oceana Commanding Officer Dies at 75." *Virginian-Pilot,* June 13, 1998.

Stover, Charles. "A Quiet Change Comes to a City." *Virginian-Pilot,* September 8, 1969.

Swift, Earl, and Jack Dorsey. "As the Navy's Jets Have Gotten Bigger and Louder, Businesses and Homes Have Crept Closer to Oceana and Fentress Airfields." *Virginian-Pilot*, May 3, 1998.

Tazewell, Calvert Walke. "Family Underground: A Record of Tazewell and Allied Families Burial Blots." Virginia Beach, VA: W.S. Dawson, August 1991.

————. "Gleanings on Walke Family Homes." Virginia Beach, VA: W.S. Dawson Company, November 1988.

Thisdell, Roberta. "Dome, Sweet Dome: Virginia Beach Landmark Goes Out with a Blast of Nostalgic Rock and Lots of Memories." *Virginian-Pilot,* June 30, 1993.

Tucker, George Holbert. *Virginian-Pilot*, November 26, 1950, and March 18, 1956.

————. "Tidewater Landfalls: The Cemetery Flashed On." *Virginian-Pilot*, March 18, 1974.

————. "What Happened Here." *Virginian-Pilot*, May 1969.

Virginia Beach Sun. "All that Remains of Fairfield." June 22, 1972.

————. "Fairfield Will Go." March 2, 1972.

————. "Old Fairfield House to Be Demolished." February 17, 1972.

Virginian-Pilot. "Archaeological Dig Is Planned at Farm." March 12, 1987.

————. "Arts Center to Get Historic Farmhouse." March 11, 1987.

————. "Beach Dig's Mysteries to Be Tapped: Experts to Work Despite Lack of Time and Money." April 10, 1989.

———. "Builder Invites Archaeological Study." March 19, 1987.

———. "Farm Land Gives Way to Luxury Dwellings." June 18, 1988.

———. "Ferry Farm's Owner Blocks Archaeologist." March 18, 1987.

———. "Life's Film Ends for Charlie Borjes, Good Photographer, Good Citizen." May 24, 1959.

———. "Timeline: Oceana's Brush with BRAC." May 25, 2006.

———. "Virginia Beach's Green Line: Should the Line Hold?" August 21, 1996, editorial.

Virginian-Pilot and Ledger-Star. "Fairfield's Appreciation Substantial." November 7, 1982.

———. "Poplar Hall Grounds Could Be Hiding Archaeological Gems, Local Woman Says." March 18, 1984.

———. "Progress Crowds Fabled Farmhouse." March 7, 1987.

White, Benjamin Dey. "Gleanings in the History of Princess Anne County." *Virginian-Pilot and Norfolk Landmark*, August 12, 13, 14, 15 and 16, 1924.

RECOMMENDED READING

While some of the books listed here were published long ago, the Old Dominion University Patricia W. and J. Douglas Perry Library, Virginia Wesleyan College Henry Clay Hofheimer II Library, Princess Anne/Virginia Beach Historical Society, Norfolk Historical Society, Norfolk County Historical Society and local public libraries often have available circulating and archival copies.

Beverley, Robert. *The History and Present State of Virginia.* Chapel Hill: University of North Carolina Press, 1947. Original volume first published in London, 1705.

Brien, Thomas M., and Oliver Diefendorf. *General Orders of the War Department Embracing the Years 1861, 1862 and 1863 Adapted Specifically for the Use of the Army and Navy of the United States in Two Volumes*. Vol. 2. New York: Derby and Miller, 1864.

Dunn, Joseph, and Barbara Lyle. *Virginia Beach "Wish You Were Here."* Virginia Beach, VA: Donning, 1983.

Forrest, William S. *Historical and Descriptive Sketches of Norfolk and Vicinity*. Philadelphia, PA: Lindsay and Blakiston, 1853.

Haile, Edward Wright, ed. *Jamestown Narratives: Eyewitness Accounts of the Virginia Colony—The First Decade: 1607–1617*. Champlain, VA: Roundhouse, 1998.

Hariot, Thomas. *A Briefe and True Report of the New Found Land of Virginia*. London, 1588. Republished Charlottesville: University of Virginia Press, 2007.

Howe, Henry. *Historical Collections of Virginia*. Charleston, SC: Babcock and Company, 1845.

Jordan, Frederick S., and James Matthias IV. *Virginia Beach: A Pictorial History*. Richmond, VA: Thomas F. Hale, 1974.

Jordan, John Woolf. *Genealogical and Personal History of the Allegheny Valley Pennsylvania*. Vol. 2. New York: Lewis Historical Publishing Company, 1913.

Kellam, Sadie Scott, and Vernon Hope. *Old Houses in Princess Anne, Virginia*. Portsmouth, VA: Printcraft Press, 1931.

Kyle, Louisa Venable. *The History of Eastern Shore Chapel and Lynnhaven Parish 1642–1969*. Norfolk, VA: Teagle and Little, 1969.

Lewis, Clifford M., and Albert J. Loomie. *The Spanish Jesuit Mission in Virginia, 1570–1572*. Chapel Hill: University of North Carolina Press, 1953.

Mansfield, Stephen S. *Princess Anne County and Virginia Beach: A Pictorial History*. Virginia Beach, VA: Donning, 1991.

Mason, George Carrington. *Colonial Churches in Tidewater Virginia*. Richmond, VA: Whittet and Shepperson, 1945.

McIntosh, Charles F. *Lower Norfolk County and Norfolk County Wills, 1637–1710*. Richmond, Virginia, 1914. Reprint Easley, SC: Southern Historical Press, 1982.

Meade, William. *Old Churches, Ministers and Families of Virginia*. Vol. 1. Philadelphia, PA: J.B. Lippincott, 1891.

Porter, John W.H. *History of Norfolk County, Virginia, 1861–65*. Portsmouth, VA: W.A. Fiske, Printer and Bookbinder, 1892.

Stewart, William H., Colonel, ed. *History of Norfolk County and Representative Citizens, 1637–1900*. Chicago, IL: Biography Publishing Company, 1902.

Tigner, James, Jr. *Greetings from Virginia Beach*. Atglen, PA: Schiffer Publishing, 2008.

Virginia Beach Public Library. *The Beach: A History of Virginia Beach, Virginia*. Virginia Beach, VA: Department of Public Libraries, 1996.

Wichard, Rogers Dey. *The History of Lower Tidewater Virginia*. 3 vols. New York: Lewis Historical Publishing Company, 1959.

Yarsinske, Amy Waters. *The Elizabeth River*. Charleston, SC: The History Press, 2007.

———. *The Martin Years—Norfolk Will Always Remember Roy*. Gloucester Point, VA: Hallmark Publishing, 2001.

———. *Mud Flats to Master Jet Base: Fifty Years at NAS Oceana*. Gloucester Point, VA: Hallmark Publishing, 2001.

————. *A Story in Development: The First 100 Years of S.L. Nusbaum Realty Company*. Virginia Beach, VA: Donning, 2009.

————. *Summer on the Southside*. Charleston, SC: Arcadia Publishing, 1998.

————. *Virginia Beach: A History of Virginia's Golden Shore*. Charleston, SC: Arcadia Publishing, 2002.

————. *Virginia Beach: Jewel Resort of the Atlantic*. Charleston, SC: Arcadia Publishing, 1998.

INDEX

About the Author

A nationally known, award-winning author of narrative nonfiction, Amy Waters Yarsinske received her master of planning degree from the University of Virginia School of Architecture and her bachelor of arts degrees in English and economics from Randolph-Macon Woman's College. She is a former president of the Norfolk Historical Society, cofounder of the Norfolk Historical Foundation and a graduate of CIVIC Leadership Institute. Yarsinske has over two decades of experience in the publishing industry as an author and editor and has made repeated appearances as a guest and commentator for major media, including American and foreign networks and international, national and regional radio markets. She is a member of Investigative Reporters and Editors (IRE), Authors Guild and American Society of Journalists and Authors (ASJA). She is the author of fifty-five books of nonfiction, including the widely read, award-winning *No One Left Behind: The Lt. Comdr. Michael Scott Speicher Story* (Dutton/NAL, 2002 and 2003; Listen and Live Audio, 2002, 2004 and 2006; Topics Entertainment, 2004; Listen and Live MP3, 2007; and Playaway Digital Audio Player, 2009).

Many years ago, Yarsinske made a commitment to tell the story of the Old Dominion one book at a time, and most especially "America's First Region," which includes the cities and counties of Hampton Roads and northeastern North Carolina. The author is a Hampton Roads native whose maternal grandfather's family history can be traced to the very beginning of what is today the city of Virginia Beach, to the first men and women of the Lynnhaven Parish, Lower Norfolk County, and to the later establishment of Princess Anne County and the first resort that sprang up on Virginia's golden shore.

Visit us at

www.historypress.net